DRESSAGE

DRESSAGE

Training and Exercises
for Competition

Léonie Marshall

B.T. Batsford Ltd · London

First published 1993

© Léonie Marshall, 1993

All rights reserved. No part of this publication
may be reproduced, in any form or by any means,
without permission from the Publisher

Typeset by Servis Filmsetting Ltd, Manchester
and printed in Great Britain by
Butler & Tanner Ltd, Frome

Published by
B.T. Batsford Ltd
4 Fitzhardinge Street
London W1H 0AH

A CIP catalogue record for this book is available
from the British Library

ISBN 0 7134 6958 7

CONTENTS

I should like to dedicate this book to the horses, especially Oberon, Orion, Othello and Octavia and to my first Riding Master, the late Lt Col Jack Hance.

ACKNOWLEDGEMENTS

I should like to give special thanks to my husband, Barry, Pauline Snelson and Sylvia Sullivan for their help in getting the show on the road! My thanks to Carole Vincer for the technical line illustrations; Gabrielle Ceriden Morse for the decorative line illustrations; Stuart and Christine Newsham for photographs 1, 2, 3, 6, 7, 10, 12, 13, 15, 19b and c, 26 and 28; Ann Sagar for 8; and Bob Langrish for photographs 4, 5, 9, 11, 14, 16, 18a and b, 19a, 20, 21, 22a and b, 23, 24, 25, 27 and 29. Also thanks to David Hamer for 17.

There are numerous others who wittingly or unwittingly have contributed to this work. They include a large number of the world's leading exponents of the art, both equine and human. In addition to these experts, so much knowledge has also been derived from my dozens of pupils who over a long period have taught me so much!

For the sake of clarity, the horse is referred to as 'he', the rider as 'he' or 'she', and the dressage judge as 'she' throughout the text.

Part 1
THE DRESSAGE HORSE AND RIDER

1

WHAT IS DRESSAGE?

Dressage is the systematic training of the horse and rider by means of exercises so that they can perform as a partnership to the best of their ability in whatever sphere they choose.

Training is a matter of degree. In its simplest form, it is going forward, stopping and turning in a balanced, controlled way – something which all riders should be able to achieve for the sake of safety and the pleasure of both parties. In its highest form, dressage is a classical art. Between the two extremes lies every variation of degree.

Although it should be artistic, dressage is also a science. Good riders realise the necessity of a thorough knowledge of the horse's structure, the way the skeleton is constructed, its locomotive capabilities and limitations. They understand the horse's muscular, nervous and digestive systems, and the influence of the horse's senses and its power of memory.

They learn how to train horses of varying temperaments and types, how to influence the horse through the rider's position and aids, how exercises develop the horse's physique and mentality. They learn how to use equipment, to understand cause and effect, know when to pressure the horse and when to ease off. In addition, they will know what a judge is looking for at the different levels of dressage tests and be able to assess their work accurately (1).

The Greek statesman, Xenophon, and subsequent masters placed much importance on the principle of systematic work to produce a riding horse that would be quiet, supple and obedient, pleasant to look at and comfortable to ride.

Xenophon, on the training of a war-horse, says: 'If you desire to handle a good war-horse so as to make his action the more magnificent and striking you must refrain from pulling at his mouth with the bit as well as from whipping and spurring him', also, he goes on to say if this is done, horses will behave badly 'that are fretted by their riders into ugly or ungraceful action but if you teach a horse to go with a light hand on the bit and yet hold his head well up and to arch his neck you will be making him just what the animal himself glories and delights in!'

We may not be riding war-horses but these comments seem very appropriate to the dressage horse of the present day. So often riders make their horses look ugly by ignorant or unsympathetic riding and by using forceful methods which take away the horse's natural pride and carriage (2).

Training a horse is a great responsibility as well as a challenge. The objectives must be kept in mind throughout training, the principles adhered to. It takes a long

time to produce a masterpiece but a crafts-man does not resent the months and years he spends diligently putting in the details until his efforts are rewarded.

The thrills of dressage are rare and transitory as the struggle to achieve the right feel eludes you. The greatest thrills come from having struggled and suc-ceeded, especially on a horse you have trained yourself. The incentive to begin often comes from seeing a top rider per-forming on a beautiful horse making it all look so easy! The will to continue comes from within, as interest in the subject takes a grip. If competition is the aim, the desire to win will drive you through the

1 An 'in hand' show horse – this picture demonstrates some good points of conformation: the good front with the neck rising from the wither to an arched crest; a sloping shoulder necessary to freedom and scope of stride; a short back with rounded barrel and strong hind-quarters; and strong forearms, second thighs and joints combining with strong cannons and plenty of bone. Any horse will perform better if fit and well and it is particularly important for a dressage horse to look attractive

troubles you encounter, but dressage is not simply about winning, it is also about discovering how to perform as a partner-ship and it is often this discovery which brings about the deepest satisfaction and fulfilment **(3)**.

2 *(Opposite)* Successful event horse Mystic Minstrel ridden by Rachael Bayliss. A good example of a straight horse with the rider sitting extremely well and looking where she is going

3 *(Above)* Robert Oliver riding a hack at the Royal Show. This illustrates a different type of horse also suitable for dressage and showing very good conformation. The rider is taking the reins in one hand to show the easy control he has over the horse which proves it is well trained and mannered. Although a more lightly built horse the same correct points of conformation are present

2

THE DRESSAGE HORSE

Finding a suitable horse is especially important if one has competitions in mind. For those who want to enjoy their riding at home and want to train for their own amusement, the make and shape of their horse is not so important a consideration, although it must be said that the better the horse's conformation, the easier it will be for both horse and rider. Almost any horse can be improved, even if it has conformation faults or a temperament problem, but why make the task harder for oneself by choosing something with obvious difficulties?

Sometimes, for financial reasons, we have to settle for animals which are less than ideal, but we can still choose the best available.

A knowledge of conformation is not only desirable for the competitive rider but an actual necessity if he is to evaluate potential. A horse that is built on the wrong lines may have problems with action, balance, collection, extension and so on. Also, it may not present an attractive picture. The overall picture is what the judge will see even before you start the test, so in order to create the right impression, the horse should be as attractive as possible.

Types of Horse

First of all, consider the type of horse you would like. There are so many that it can be difficult to decide and, of course, there is the financial aspect, but all types have their own qualities and attributes.

Warmblood

Warmblood horses are popular worldwide and are successful dressage horses (4). They generally look impressive, being of sizeable stature. They have good action, with plenty of scope and, normally, their temperament is placid so they are not easily upset or disturbed by the pressures of training. Their disadvantage, if one can call it that, is that they can be too big and scopey for novice riders or anyone who lacks height or length of leg. Their size can make for difficulties negotiating a small arena. A small person may find themselves so unequal in strength that, however good a rider, they are simply not able to keep sufficient control. This control is not just a question of being able to stop when required but more a question of being able to engage the hindquarters sufficiently and bring the horse together.

4 Ferdi Eilberg riding at the Goodwood dressage competition on a warmblood, the type now most commonly used by top dressage riders

5 Diana Mason's horse Prince Consort. Some Anglo-Arabs tend to be more towards the pure Arabian and others not, but the combination of the Arab alertness, spirit and head (with a dish and a lovely large eye), and the correct conformation and strength of the English breeds makes a very attractive picture

Arab

Arab horses can be full of an ethereal beauty. With their lovely, dished heads, large eyes, ears pricked to pick up the smallest noise, and expressions full of curiosity, they are full of interest in life as they float along with their spectacular action. Sadly, even with all this magic, they are rarely suitable for dressage to a high competitive level. This is not to say that they cannot do the work, but their inherited independence often makes total obedience a problem. In addition, they lack height, and, most importantly, their action tends to be rather straight-legged for dressage competition, where a more rounded action is preferred.

Anglo-arabs or partbred Arabs can be just as lovely to look at and sometimes have an attractive, light-footed action, yet with better bending of the joints than the pure-bred Arab (5). Because of the variance in their parentage, the size and type cannot be defined. Suffice to say that there have been very successful dressage horses of this breeding.

Thoroughbred

Many people train Thoroughbreds and, if they have the right temperament, they make a lovely picture with their classical lines and graceful movement (6). Unfortunately, a great many become too tense under the pressures of training. They also need time to mature physically. They have great powers of learning but do need patient and careful training.

Cross-bred

There are many cross-bred horses that are very suitable for the job and as many that are not. Thoroughbred mares crossed with a draught horse or vice versa may produce a heavy type with limited action, which would not be suitable, but having said that, breeding can produce the most unlikely results, so nothing can be stated categorically.

A proven cross is the Thoroughbred with a Welsh Cob (7). There have been a large number of very successful horses in dressage with this breeding, though again they can vary enormously. The good ones combine the beauty of the Thoroughbred with the activity of the Cob. As both varieties have a quick intelligence and reaction to situations, they may need extra patience during training.

Welsh Cobs themselves are not generally used for top dressage but there are Cobs of the lightweight show type, which, if they move well, can be quite successful, though rarely will they have the scope for top class competition.

Lipizzaner

The Lipizzaner has, of course, been used for dressage for many years and has a spectacular appearance and strength especially for the airs above the ground (8), perfect in the context of the wonderful displays of the Spanish Riding School in Vienna. Some Lipizzaners have been very successful in international competition but against the bigger, more scopey horses they can seem limited.

Conformation

Whatever is the horse of your choice, there are some basic points that should apply to all. Although I have tended to refer to the horse as 'he', this implies no preference, for mares can be as successful as geldings and stallions.

First of all, the horse should be the right size for you, as it is no good being under or over-horsed. The scope of the stride can present difficulties. If a horse with a very

6 Though thoroughbreds can often be temperamental and highly strung, Wily Trout, ridden here by Christopher Bartle, is a former event horse which became an extremely successful international dressage horse, proving that thoroughbreds can hold their own in this discipline

7 *(Above)* Miranda Morley on Omega – this horse is showing a good stance (outline) although the rider's body is slightly behind the vertical

8 Lipizzaner

big, springy stride is asked to go forwards as he really should, it is quite hard to sit to the stride as is required in most tests. A small rider will have more trouble than a taller or larger person, who at least has the advantage of being able to wrap his legs around the horse.

Of course, learning to 'sit into' a horse with a big stride in trot is a technique, but nevertheless, it can be extremely hard work. A rangy canter can also cause the less experienced rider considerable heart-ache as he struggles to bring the horse together. Placid temperaments are certainly preferable to ones that are tense or anxious but a big, placid horse does need motivating: the effort involved can be exhausting for the rider.

The horse should be attractive to look at – no-one really wants to watch a cart-horse clomping round a dressage arena – but beware of buying something just because it is beautiful! It would be a good thing if he had a reasonably well-shaped head that is the right size for his body. His ears should neither be enormous nor lop. His neck should rise from the withers arching into a good crest, with plenty of room where it joins the head by the jowel. His shoulders should slope well to give maximum freedom of movement. His back should be short rather than long and his hindquarters should be strong over the loin.

His body should be supported by strong limbs which are four-square under him and have strength in the forearm and thigh. The joints should be well formed with short cannons to sloping but not overlong pasterns. The feet, of utmost importance, should match each other, be round in shape and house well-grown healthy frogs.

Action

Ideal conformation is hard to find but action is of equal importance. The gaits should all show free, generous strides that cover the ground. In walk, the steps should be long and easy, with the hind feet well overtracking the print left by the forefeet. In trot, the shoulders should lift the forelimbs with each step and have an in-built rhythm that shows scope and good bending of the limb joints. The canter should have natural balance and a good moment of suspension between strides.

Although unlevelness and irregularities in rhythm are normally man-made, it is important to notice any discrepancies of this nature when deciding upon a horse to train, as such faults are marked down in dressage competitions. The hind feet should clearly follow the tracks of the forefeet – essential if the horse is to be truly straight when ridden. The general cause of such faults is probably poor riding, which has allowed the horse to become stiff and one-sided. However, there are occasions when the cause can be from an injury of some kind, which it may or may not be possible to correct.

Veterinary Examination

When purchasing any horse it is normally advisable to have him checked over by a veterinary surgeon who can at least prevent you from starting with a problem. When requesting an examination, make it clear to the vet the purpose for which you require the horse.

Training a horse for dressage is a long and arduous task, so aim to start with the best material available!

3

THE RIDER

Training a dressage horse is a fascinating business, the more one learns the more there is to learn. Of course, each rider will have her own particular aim, whether modest or demanding, but certain qualities are necessary to achieve any degree of success.

Determination

Determination heads these qualities; knowing in which direction you are going and having a positive attitude to overcoming difficulties. There will be many occasions when you will feel like giving up or will look for an easier way. Like all things which are hard to attain, there is no easy route and you will have to be strong willed and single-minded, sometimes ruthless, if you want to reach your goal.

Dedication

Dedication is next on the list, for you could be easily swayed if your heart and mind are not totally engrossed in dressage. You must be prepared to school your horse each day and work for a result, not being interrupted in your concentration by any outside influences. Whether it is pouring with rain, snowing a blizzard or the sun is blazing, the horse must be ridden. You may have some injury and be in pain or be feeling as though you are about to take your last breath but very little will deter you from training. Total dedication means not only overcoming how you feel, but may also mean giving up some of life's comforts in order to pursue your sport. It is of course up to each individual to determine their degree of commitment.

If you are dedicated and determined, you will also be fully prepared to work as hard as is necessary to achieve your goal. If it means riding at six in the morning or nine in the evening with your job in-between, you will cheerfully do it. You will work hard during the time you ride, not wasting precious minutes having a breather or admiring the view. You will realise the need to be fit in mind and body to sustain effort and will, by your work, make the horse fit so that he can also cope with the effort.

Riding Well

Even with these qualities, nothing can be achieved unless you ride well: therefore, it is essential to develop a good position and firm seat from which the aids can be applied correctly.

Fig. 1 Rider in the correct position for dressage – a straight line can be imagined dropping from the rider's ear, through the hip to the ankle. Another straight line goes from the horse's mouth through to the elbow. The rider's weight is evenly distributed over both seat bones

The first prerequisite of good riding is to develop a deep seat which enables you to sit close to the horse at all times **(Fig.1)**. Riding without stirrups is probably the best way to learn, as the muscles can develop strongly without the hindrance of the stirrups and the movement of the horse is easier to follow. It is important to relax the seat muscles to allow yourself into the saddle, and to have the inside of the thigh flat against the saddle flap. Some people have to pay more attention to this, especially those with thicker than average thighs. The heels should be lower than the toes or may be level but the ankle must not be stiff.

The position of the seat cannot be maintained unless the body is upright. It must not be held rigidly but must be supple and follow the horse's movement. If you allow your back to be slack or rounded, you will lose the correct position of the seat and legs, and thus the influence of the aids. The head should be upright on the spine as any undue nodding, tilting sideways or looking down may affect the straightness of the spine which then affects everything else. The arms should be held in a relaxed fashion round the body with a straight line from the elbow through the reins to the horse's mouth. There must be no tension as this will only serve to restrict the forward movement. The arms should be allowed to move as they follow the movement of the horse's head and neck but this movement only happens as a result of having asked the horse to accept the aids. This 'allowing' action of the arm is for the purpose of maintaining freedom and forward movement and does not mean that the reins should be loosened although they may be lengthened for a specific movement. The fingers must be pliable and able to feel the horse's mouth in a conversational manner, asking and responding immediately by an easing of pressure when the horse yields to the bit.

Feel

The most important attribute for any rider is to have natural feel for what his horse is doing under him **(9)**. Some riders do not possess this gift and have to learn by developing technique. Those with natural ability also need technique but will automatically sit correctly and will have an instant rapport with the horse. Sympathy and understanding of the horse, will come easily to them. They will be aware of his needs, reactions, physical and mental comfort. They will feel without being taught when something is right or pick up what they need to know with minimal tuition. Those who do not have such good natural aptitude need not despair. Determination and hard work will be the key to their success. It may take a little longer, but often the result is equally satisfactory.

9 Trish Gardiner demonstrates the classical riding position. Note the good line from elbow to hand through the rein to the horse's mouth; also the position of the leg, well round the horse and with the heel slightly lower than the toe but not exaggerated. The seat is well into the saddle with the body upright. Horse and rider are very much in balance and harmony with each other

The Aids

The rider's ability to feel and assess his horse's movement is equalled in importance by the ability to communicate well via the aids. There are a basic set of rules for this communication which, if adhered to properly, make the process simple. These are as follows; the rider's legs used simultaneously should make the horse go straight forwards. The hands control that forward energy. The seat and weight of the rider, and the voice assist the legs and hands. To 'break down' the use of the aids further, each hand and leg has a specific part to play. The rider's inside leg has the added responsibility of maintaining or increasing impulsion and making and holding the bend of the horse's body. The outside leg assists the inside leg with the impulsion and controls the hindquarters. The inside rein achieves the flexion and direction while the outside rein controls the speed. Both control the forehand. Here are a few examples of aids for specific movements to show the consistency of these basics with some additions where necessary, i.e.:

Shoulder-in

The inside leg asks for and maintains the bend and also keeps the horse going forwards.
The outside leg keeps the hindquarters round the inside leg and helps maintain angle and energy.
The inside rein keeps the flexion and directs the angle.
The outside rein controls the speed and impulsion and assists the inside rein in maintaining the angle.

Canter strike-off

The inside leg asks for and maintains the bend and keeps the horse going forwards.

In addition it asks for the strike-off when required.
The outside leg keeps the hindquarters round the inside leg, helps with 'positioning for canter' and lets the horse know which leg he is required to strike-off with. The inside rein keeps the flexion and shows the horse which direction to go in. The outside rein controls the speed and collection, and helps with the 'positioning'.

Legs

Although the aids have a basic structure as described, there must be small variations of leg pressure for the horse to differentiate between certain movements. There are also minor differences in the outside leg position between, for example, half pass and canter strike-off, but these differences are very small and each rider will have his own arrangements with his horse based on the laid down principles. The arrangements, providing they are consistent, will be part of the partnership between horse and rider.

Remember that the use of the legs should come before the hands in all movements, including halts, rein-back and all transitions, where there is a temptation primarily to use the reins. If the horse's hindquarters are not kept engaged by the rider's legs, impulsion, which is the first basic necessity in successful riding, will dwindle, and any control by the hands will serve to halt the impulsion further. The use of the legs should be such that, from a contact with the horse's sides they successfully influence him. This 'contact' may be firm, less firm, squeezing or still but should be maintained quietly with no gripping by the calves to balance the rider nor ugly kicking. The leg aids should be so subtle as to be almost invisible to the onlooker. This result only comes from patient training (10). The horse is helped to understand by, initially, the rider's voice, repetition of exercises, and a schooling whip used correctly. Never use the whip for punishment but only to reinforce the legs.

Hands

Similarly, a 'contact' must be maintained with the horse's mouth. This 'contact' asks him to yield and accept the bit and may have to be used in varying ways to get him to do this. A horse does not naturally have a 'good mouth'. It has to be made. There is a misconception that if a young horse stops or turns easily that he has a naturally 'soft' mouth. It is far more likely that that is what he wanted to do anyway! A made or good mouth is the result of properly co-ordinated aids which ask the horse to go forwards and then control him by the correct use of the bit. The 'contact' by the hands will only be acceptable to the horse if they are sympathetic, consistent, can feel resistance and overcome it, and can ease rein tension at the moment when the horse has properly responded. If the hands hold the reins in a 'dead' grip, the horse's mouth will also be dead. The fingers should be able to apply pressure through the reins to the bit by a feel and ease method which may sometimes be equal, alternate, or one rein used several times more than the other (for instance, in trying to persuade a stiff horse to yield to a particular side). At any rate, they should 'talk' to the horse's mouth and make themselves understood by praising the horse and responding with a sympathetic feel when he answers. The rider should feel relaxation of the poll and the lower jaw of the horse and possibly some gentle chewing movement which helps saliva-

10 A rider being lunged for the purpose of developing a secure seat. Note that the rider's hands are rather high and the lower leg is forward

tion. Usually, when a horse works correctly he will have a 'wet' mouth or in other words plenty of white froth round his mouth but if he is cheating it will be dry. Maintaining a 'contact' is difficult for the novice rider but is so important for the horse as it is very muddling to him to have a tight rein one minute and a loose one the next. It is also impossible ever to give the aids properly in this circumstance. During training 'contact' may become more pliable as the horse becomes supple, is more impulsive or collected. It also may increase in firmness as more impulsion is created, but, whatever happens, only a horse held correctly by the 'contact' of leg and hand will ever be able to perform to a high standard.

DIAGONALS

One of the rider's duties is to develop the physical strength of the horse equally on both reins. Work should be directed so that whatever exercise is required, the horse will be able to perform without stiffness. Remember to work on both reins, obtaining a good result on both.

Something that does cause one-sidedness is if the rider fails to change his diagonal when rising in trot. The diagonals are the sequence of footfalls in trot, i.e. one pair of diagonal legs and then the other coming to the ground – off fore, near hind – near fore, off hind (a two-time beat) so the rider will rise when one pair of legs is on the ground and sit when the other pair are on the ground.

Many horses will feel more comfortable if the rider sits on one particular diagonal. Because of this the rider tends automatically to choose it each time. Eventually, the horses back muscles are strengthened on one side more than the other, causing stiffness. Therefore, it is necessary when changing the rein in rising trot, also to change the diagonal.

Weight

The use of the seat and weight should be invisible to the onlooker, as if the rider has a good depth of seat combined with suppleness, its influence will happen almost automatically if the other aids are given correctly. There may be a few occasions when the rider should sit a little more to the inside, such as in half-pass, pirouette or canter strike-off but too much alteration can be a hindrance. As a basis, the rider's weight should be distributed evenly over both seat bones.

Voice

The voice is invaluable in helping the horse to understand the aids when he is young, or to chide him or praise him during training, but as it is not allowed in a competition, you must not rely on it.

Study

The rider bears a huge responsibility in the training of his chosen horse. He must accrue the depth of knowledge necessary to take on the task and be able to be both sympathetic and firm. He must realise that praise in response to correct answers to his questions is the route to progress. He should study by watching the world's experts at work not just in the arena, but during their preparation and, if he gets the chance, in their home surroundings. Fortunately, video recordings have made many riders' work much more accessible. He must read books on the subject studying carefully different techniques so that he can build up a picture for himself. Finally he must learn from experience what works and what doesn't, what improves and what destroys. Only time and many hours of practice will do this.

4
FITNESS OF HORSE AND RIDER

The subjects of feeding and fitness are as important for the dressage horse, as they are for any other top class competition horse. There are no hard and fast rules because circumstances and conditions vary so much, but here are some guidelines to follow.

Feeding

Age of horse

First of all, the age of the horse should be taken into account. A young horse, for example, may or may not have had a good start in life. If he has, he will not need building-up in condition prior to beginning his ridden life although he will need to become fit for the work. If he is in poor condition, it would be unfair to set him to work until his physique is improved and indeed damage to the skeleton or muscular system sometimes occurs as a result of lack of condition or fitness. Dressage is very demanding on the horse's physical strength, particularly when carrying the unaccustomed weight of a rider. However, it can be a mistake to give too high a proportion of short feed to a young or just broken horse in an effort to build him up. He may then feel too full of himself, unable to concentrate on the rather slow, steady work required of him. Instead of co-operating, he may become too exuberant, causing problems for himself and his rider. Any resistance resulting from freshness can develop into nappiness, which can be so difficult to overcome. Therefore, a sensible programme of feeding should be planned, with the accent upon bulk food such as hay and smaller amounts of 'short feed' such as oats or horse-nuts. Supplements can be added if necessary, but if in doubt a consultation with a veterinary surgeon and perhaps a blood test could supply the answer to any deficiency.

Older horses need a sensible diet for the same reasons although the mere fact that they already probably been ridden for some time means that they should have developed a certain physical strength. A horse that has been ridden incorrectly and developed the wrong muscles may need 'letting down' for a while until his system relaxes, removing unwanted tensions. Then he may be brought to condition again slowly and, if ridden in the right way, the muscle system should come into proper use.

Size and temperament

Clearly, feeding also depends on the size of the horse involved. Theoretically, a large horse should eat a good deal more food than a smaller one. Sometimes, however, a large horse is an exceptionally good doer and needs a relatively small amount of food to keep him well covered, whereas a smaller horse may be a fussy feeder that loses condition easily. These are situations when a check by a veterinary surgeon, a good worming programme or change of diet may make the difference and everything should be considered. The temperament of each individual horse must also determine the feeding pattern. It would be foolish to pack oats into an excitable horse or to avoid giving them to a lazy one. Each horse will need his own food ratios and only trial and error may determine the most satisfactory answer. Common sense, combined with study of the subject, should eventually bring a conclusion

Fitness

Schooling in itself is hard work for a horse (and rider) as the exercise in a limited area makes the entire muscle and skeletal systems function to a high degree. This is exactly the object but to be able to work in this way the horse must be fit. Your feeding programme should bring him to a condition where he may be asked to work and then the training programme makes him fit enough to do what the rider desires. As he becomes fitter, the horse will use more energy, so the proportion of concentrates to hay increases. Fitness is only achieved by gradual means and slow steady work, giving everything time to develop (11).

Any sign of weakness over the loins or in the second thigh should be viewed with great caution as any attempt to hurry the work could easily strain these areas, causing permanent damage. Joints, if unprotected by strong muscles, can become weak. Many irregularities of stride stem from incorrect or hurried training.

If systematic training and basic principles are adhered to, the progression to advanced work, is natural not forced, and the horse is never asked to perform an exercise for which he is physically unprepared. Meanwhile, the rider will also have become fit. Work in the school will have brought this about. Many people ask whether they should adopt a fitness programme round the roads or galloping the horse occasionally. I really believe that just as the ballet dancer does not go marathon running, success comes from consolidating your work.

The ideal yard

My ideal yard and working arrangements would incorporate a covered way from house to stables, which would be enclosed, but have top doors to the outside as well so that horses could see out. The stables would have direct access to an indoor school. An indoor lungeing ring would be very useful, together with an outdoor all-weather arena of Olympic size (60 × 20 m) (Fig.2).

The realities are that most people count themselves lucky if they have an all weather outdoor school of 40 × 20 m (Fig.3). Over the years, some riders have produced horses of international standard with arenas of small proportions or even without a proper arena at all. At the very least, try to rope off an area that you can use as a school, and invest in a set of arena letters.

11 A well-muscled horse – the result of systematic training which here has developed the horse particularly along the crest, over the back and loins and in the hind-quarters

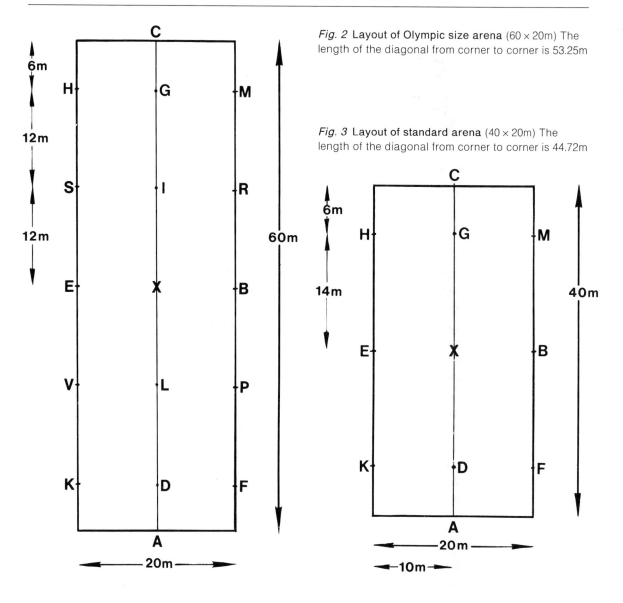

Fig. 2 Layout of Olympic size arena (60 × 20m) The length of the diagonal from corner to corner is 53.25m

Fig. 3 Layout of standard arena (40 × 20m) The length of the diagonal from corner to corner is 44.72m

5
DRESSAGE FOR THE YOUNG RIDER

The increased popularity of dressage is nowadays reflected in the number of young riders who are interested in the sport. Those who have started schooling their ponies and competing in tests have become keen to learn more and often perform better than the adults! The 'grown-ups' used to feel that very young riders should not be encouraged to specialise as there are so many other avenues open to them. However, as with all things, it is up to each individual to choose, and those youngsters who have become involved in dressage are as dedicated and hard working as anyone. It all depends on whether you want to win prizes! This is an incentive for most people, especially the young. It may not be the whole reason because there are many who do not ever enter a competition, but merely like to ride a well-trained horse, and it is now accepted that basic dressage is the correct foundation for all riding. However, we all like to go home with a 'ribbon' if we have been to a show. It is the reward for hard work and, if the judge has liked your performance, you will start the next stage with greater enthusiasm.

Young people can be very determined and are not easily intimidated by the pressures of competition. Happily, they are unaware of the politics behind the scenes, which sometimes psychologically affect their older counterparts, and they do not have added distractions of earning a living and all the responsibilities of an adult. These outside influences should be put aside when competing but that may be a lot easier said than done and it is a good deal simpler to forget school examinations than pass over in your mind those pressing bills! Concentration and devotion to the job in hand is so necessary to success. This is hard for anyone especially very young riders. It will be a special person who has the ability to give themselves entirely.

Because dressage competitions vary from relatively easy stages to the very difficult, each rider can choose the level for which he or she wants to aim. Because the first stages are based on simple exercises that are the foundation for all sensible riding, other activities can easily be combined. This applies to all forms of the sport but eventing and show jumping in particular, and even games benefit from correct riding and schooling.

Children and indeed other riders often begin in a riding school, where, if they are fortunate, they will be taught to sit well, understand the aids, learn the reasons for correct riding, develop a firm seat by work without stirrups and on the lunge, and be able to ride both in and out of doors on a variety of ponies. As they progress, they may be able to ride a bigger horse to learn the feel of the stride and the extra requirements needed to control a larger animal. Lessons on a schooled horse will be exciting and useful in learning to refine the aids and will give the opportunity to practise more difficult movements.

Choosing a Pony

Choosing a pony for dressage is not easy and much depends on the ability of the rider **(12)**. To over-horse a young rider is a huge mistake as at best the experience is confidence-sapping, at worst an accident could put him or her off for life, so although the aim may be to win at 'the top', ambitious parents must beware of jumping in at the deep end, it may be wiser to paddle through shallow water first! The enormous range of types of ponies can be extremely confusing but the action and conformation of the pony will play a big part in its chances of success, so should be assessed carefully. Its size and age must be taken into consideration, together with its suitability, particularly in regard to temperament.

12 A suitable dressage pony

Trainers

Having chosen the animal, time should be given to allow child and pony to really get to know each other. A trainer will need to be found and one who has had personal experience of top class competition will help the really ambitious child to succeed.

Sometimes the combination of rider/ trainer does not 'click'. In this event, no amount of cajoling will produce a satisfactory result; it is better for everyone if another trainer is sought.

Parental Responsibilities

Being the parent of an ambitious child can be extremely testing. The combination of encouragement with control is exceedingly difficult. The child must not be precocious or proud, and yet must have confidence in her prowess and not be nervous in public. Coolness in the arena is an essential element for any test rider and although this quality can be cultivated to an extent by practice and experience, if it is naturally in the temperament, it is an enormous advantage. Parents can be a big help to their children if they give the right sort of support. Obviously, financial support is a major factor: and the right pony, clothes, lessons, tack, and transport can mean considerable financial outlay. Parents also give essential help on the ground and at shows. Running down the judges in front of children should obviously be avoided. Complaining loudly in the Secretary's Office or being unpleasant to either the child or the pony are faults which I am afraid are all too common in parental attitudes. It is hard being a parent in normal circumstances but under the spotlights everything is accentuated, observed and noted and many a budding star has fallen because of the wrong kind of behaviour either by himself or his family.

Having said all that, of course the young rider is the potential star of the future and is not only welcome in competition, but vitally important. Any help which is offered either by trainers, judges or other competitors should be thankfully received and if not actually acted upon, at least analysed to find possible means for improvements.

On the whole, I have found that the majority of young riders and even quite small children can, with help, achieve an agreeably high standard training their ponies themselves. There will be those, however, who do need extra assistance from an adult who can school the pony for them. An experienced rider may be necessary to teach obedience and control to a strong pony, or to improve a pony's balance, collection, or understanding of the aids. However, it is important that the child takes part as much as possible, so that he feels it is his own achievement and, more significantly, so that he learns from personal experience.

Part 2
BASIC
TRAINING

6

TERMS AND TESTS

The Language of Dressage

Throughout the following chapters certain words and phrases are used frequently. Dressage is full of terms that may seem strange to the uninitiated, but here is a brief explanation of those which are inseparable from successful training.

The horse

Activity The elasticity of the hind legs (bending of joints) which gives the gait lift and forward movement.

Cadence Evolves from regularity and rhythm when impulsion and activity give lift and expression to the gait.

Collection The bringing together, by use of the aids, both ends of the horse, furthering greater engagement of the hindquarters, for the purpose of lifting and lightening the forehand.

Ease of movement The ability of the horse to flow without difficulty from one movement to another.

Engagement The lowering of the hindquarters, enabling the horse to bring his hind legs further under his body so that he will be better balanced and able to go forwards more easily.

Extension The greatest ground-covering stride the horse is capable of giving in each gait.

Freedom of movement Having a forward, ground-covering stride, unrestricted by the rider, achieved from impulsion and submission to the aids.

Impulsion The energy created by the hindquarters which takes the horse forwards.

Lightness Achieved from correct balance and engagement of the hindquarters, so that the forehand is lifted and able to operate without leaning on the rider's hands. (This should not be confused with a loose rein.)

Positioning Preparation for an exercise by the use of a slight shoulder-in position.

Purity of gait The correct sequence of steps in each gait, i.e. walk – four beats, trot – two beats, canter – three beats.

Regularity The exactness and equality of the steps at each gait.

Rhythm The maintenance of a precise rhythm of steps at each gait.

Self carriage The horse is able to perform in his own balance, without leaning on the rider's hands.

Straightness True straightness comes from the horse's hind legs following the track of the forelegs and from suppleness.

Submission Complete acceptance of the aids without resistance.

Suppleness A lack of resistance or stiffness in the poll, lower jaw, back and leg joints.

Tempo The slowness or quickness of the steps in each gait.

The rider

Position The maintenance of the classical position for the rider in the saddle.

Effect of aids The way the rider uses the aids and the result they have on the horse's way of going.

Tests and Requirements

National tests

The following shows the progression of national tests in both Great Britain and the USA, with details of what the horse is expected to show.

Preliminary (GB) Arena size 40 × 20 m

Training tests level 1, 2, 3, 4 (USA)
Working gaits
Progressive transitions
Straightness on centre line
Correct bend
Calmness
Smoothness of transitions
Correctness of gaits
Balance
Impulsion – desire to move forward, elasticity of steps, relaxation of back
Lightness and ease of movement
Attention and confidence
Acceptance of aids

20 m circles trot or canter
10 m half circle at walk
Lengthened strides
Serpentine on long side of arena 3 or 5 m in trot

Novice (GB) Arena size 40 × 20 m or 60 × 20 m

Training tests (USA) *as above plus:*
15 m circles in trot or canter
10 m circles and half circles in trot
Serpentines in trot
Start of rein back
Turns across school in trot
15 m half circle in canter
Lengthened canter
Give and retake the reins, trot or canter
Halt for specified number of seconds

USA tests also include leg yield in trot, and serpentine in canter without change of leg in their first level tests.

Elementary (GB) Arena size 60 × 20 m

First level (USA) Arena size 40 × 20 m *as above plus*:
10 m circles in trot and canter
Medium trot or canter
Extended trot
Shoulder-in
Greater accuracy

Second level (USA) Arena size 40 × 20 m or 60 × 20 m *also includes*:
8 m circles
Simple change of leg
Counter change
Travers
Training walk half pirouette

Third level (USA) *includes*:
Half pass
Collected walk
Half pirouette in walk

Medium (GB) *includes*:
Simple change of leg
Counter Canter
Half pass

Walk half pirouette
Extended walk, trot and canter
Collected walk, trot and canter

Advanced medium (GB)

Third level (USA) Arena size 50 × 20 m
includes:
Changes in the air
Half pirouette in canter

Advanced (lower tests) (GB)

Fourth level (USA) *includes*:
Sequence changes, four- and three-tempi
Counter changes of hand in trot and canter
Precision in all movements and to all markers

Fifth level (USA) 6 m volte included

Advanced (higher tests) (GB)
More difficult counter changes of hand in trot and canter
Rein-back see-saw
Sequence changes to single-tempi
Passage
Piaffe

International dressage – FEI tests

There are five tests at international level, supervised by the Fédération Equestre Internationale (FEI).

Prix St George has relatively easy lateral work, including shoulder-in and half-passes in trot and canter. In this test there are medium, collected and extended movements in all gaits, half-pirouettes in walk and canter, rein-back to canter, and flying changes to four- and three-time.

Intermediare I is similar in difficulty to the Prix St George but includes counter changes of hand and see-saw and flying changes to two-time.

Intermediare II leads the rider towards Grand Prix by the introduction of piaffe covering ground (one metre obligatory seven to eight steps) and seven, one-time flying changes. The remainder of the work is increased in difficulty by the use of steeper angles for lateral work, a greater number of counter changes of hand and a serpentine in canter, some flying changes being to true lead and some to counter canter. Also included are full canter pirouettes.

Grand Prix requires all the foregoing exercises in increased difficulty, plus precise steps for piaffe, passage and the transitions to and from piaffe. In addition, it calls for 15 one-time flying changes.

Grand Prix Special tests the ultimate ability of the horse in collection, impulsion, suppleness and obedience in all movements. It is normally open only to the top 12 horse and rider combinations in the Grand Prix.

Explanation of Variations within a Gait

The following variations of pace may be demanded in tests.

Working

The horse should be going well forward in a balanced, rhythmic, active and impulsive way, on a stride at which he can comfortably perform the exercises asked of him.

Collected

In collection the horse is brought more together. The stride may be shorter than in the working gait, but it should not lose any activity or impulsion, nor be restricted.

Medium

This is a larger edition of the working gait, with a longer stride and greater suspension between strides and some lowering of the hindquarters.

Extended

The maximum stride the horse can achieve, covering ground during the moment of suspension in trot and canter. The reach of the forelegs and hindlegs should match. The engagement of the hindquarters will lift the forehand, allowing the shoulders freedom. The frame will lengthen slightly.

Free walk on a long rein

The horse should walk in a natural, relaxed way on long strides, the hindfeet overtracking the prints of the forefeet. He should stretch down with his hand and neck, his nose slightly in front of the vertical. Although a contact by the rider should be maintained, the horse should have freedom of movement.

7

THE YOUNG HORSE

Having found your ideal horse, the most important thing is to first establish a relationship with it. The rapport or common ground upon which to build this relationship depends very much on the character and temperament of both partners. If you have chosen your horse partly because of his equable temperament, it is only right that you should endeavour to complement that temperament with your own calmness and patience, thus gaining his trust and willingness to please. Co-operation from the horse will only come about from understanding and this understanding will only happen if you are clear and consistent. Muddled thinking, lack of knowledge or impatience from the rider can only confuse both parties and hinder progress.

Developing a Rapport

There are two places where you can develop a relationship with the horse, in the stable and in the saddle.

In the stable

Many people do have grooms to do stable work and keep the horse smart and tidy, but I feel strongly that a partnership is closer if the rider can give some part of every day to her horse in the stable, handling him, grooming or changing rugs, tacking up and so on. Those riders who do the whole job themselves will be well aware of all the horse's idiosyncrasies, likes and dislikes. Discipline begins in the stable and the rider who knows and understands her horse on the ground and obtains obedience from him by voice or action will have an instant advantage in the saddle.

In the saddle

The attitude of the rider to the horse when mounted is of paramount importance to the development of a real rapport essential to achieve a high degree of training.

If he tries to subject the horse to a state of subservience in his attempt to command perfect obedience, he will crush the natural vitality of the horse and the performance will be dead. On the other hand, if you can work together in a mutually agreeable way, the willing response of the horse will give his performance gaiety.

Obedience

Obtaining obedience without losing vitality is very difficult and only knowledge and a great deal of patience will enable the rider to achieve it. Horses and children are very alike in their needs. Security is important, not just a roof over their heads but security from knowing they are important and wanted. They need reprimanding, sometimes strongly, but it should always be followed by reward or praise as soon as a correct response is given.

The rider has several methods of obtaining obedience from the horse when mounted: the aids, (seat, legs, hands, voice, weight), a schooling whip to help the horse to understand the meaning of the legs, and his own ability to plan, anticipate and prevent anything that might cause the horse to want to be disobedient. It is always better not to have a confrontation, which causes confusion, frustration and often anger, resulting in either or both parties being unpleasant. Working on the principle that more can be achieved through trust than violence, it is up to you to create the right situation for successful learning.

The young horse will have to accept straight away that he must not behave in an unsociable way to his rider, treading on his feet, knocking him about, nipping, kicking or any other habits which might occur to him, like a naughty child, to get his own way. Similarly, when being ridden he must go forwards when told, stop and turn. Any objects he finds frightening you must patiently help him past but never give in or allow him to evade instructions.

He must learn to accept the schooling whip, respond and go forwards or away from it. He should not be frightened of it but must nevertheless respect its authority.

Lungeing and Long-reining

The rider's voice is an essential factor and most riders will, even if they have not broken the horse themselves, wish to lunge or long-rein at some time **(Figs.4–6)**. Teaching the horse to obey the voice from the ground is very useful in helping him to

Fig. 4 Correct lungeing position – when lungeing, the trainer should be in the centre of the circle in a position where he can keep the horse going forwards. Normally, she will slightly drive the horse by moving herself on a small inner circle. This is especially the case when teaching the novice horse to lunge. An older horse who knows how to lunge may be controlled by the trainer being in a more stationary position, but at all times the trainer should be ready to move forward in order to make the horse work energetically, bend and keep a correct outline

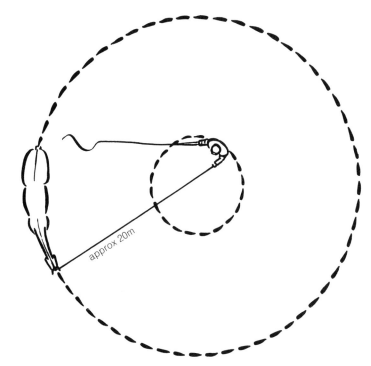

approx 20m

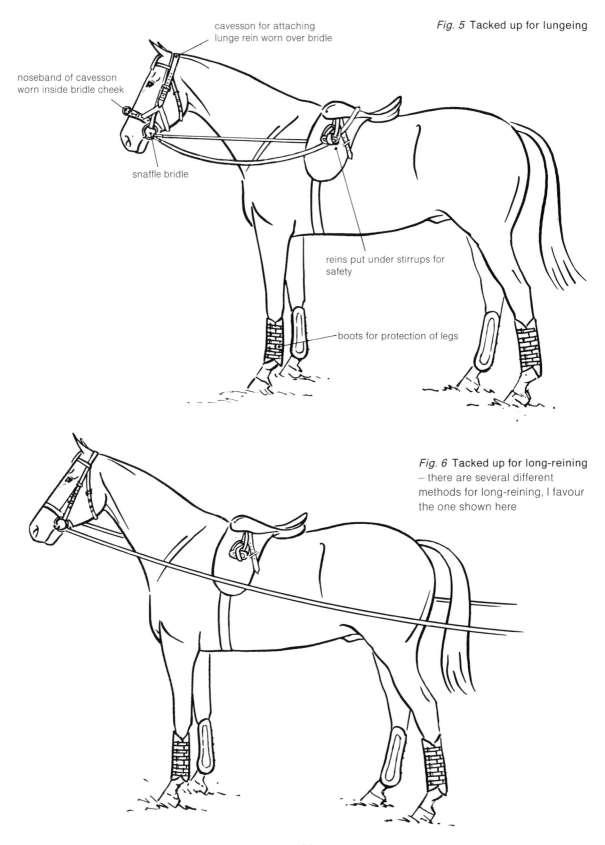

Fig. 5 Tacked up for lungeing

cavesson for attaching
lunge rein worn over bridle

noseband of cavesson
worn inside bridle cheek

snaffle bridle

reins put under stirrups for
safety

boots for protection of legs

Fig. 6 Tacked up for long-reining
– there are several different
methods for long-reining, I favour
the one shown here

comprehend the aids of the legs and hands, i.e. if the horse will walk trot and canter by word of command from the ground then these words can be used in conjunction with the aids when riding. When lungeing, the trainer should be in the centre of the circle in a position where he can keep the horse going forwards. Normally, he will slightly drive the horse by moving himself on a small inner circle. This is especially the case when teaching the novice horse to lunge. An older horse who knows how to lunge may be controlled by the trainer in a more stationary position. At all times the trainer should be ready to move forward in order to make the horse work energetically, bend and keep a correct outline.

The young horse on the lunge will learn basic control from his rider's voice, the lunge rein and the lunge whip, and he will also learn the meaning of the whip used to send him forwards **(13)**. It should never be necessary to use the whip harshly but using it correctly is a skill. The long-reins are exceedingly useful in teaching the horse to go forwards between the reins and in teaching him the feel of the bit.

Accepting the Bit

Accepting the bit must be one of the most difficult things a horse ever has to do and I have a lot of sympathy with resistance to it. At some time probably all riders have misused the bit, either knowingly as a punishment or ignorantly. Either way, it is extremely cruel and sympathy via the hands should be uppermost in every rider's mind. A young horse should have a snaffle bit firmly positioned in his mouth so that it cannot bang about and harm his teeth or gums. A correctly-fitted bit is vital and can be kept best in position by use of a flash noseband or well-fitted drop noseband (not so low that it impedes breathing) **(Figs.7–8)**. If it is possible for the horse to open his mouth or get his tongue over the bit, this will be a very bad start and may cause him always to have problems.

If the horse is driven on long-reins, he will become accustomed to the bit and its effect, and if the rider is sensible and uses his voice as well as the reins, the horse should neither become frightened of the bit nor resentful **(14)**. I would advocate the

Fig. 7 Snaffle with flash noseband

Fig. 8 Snaffle with drop noseband

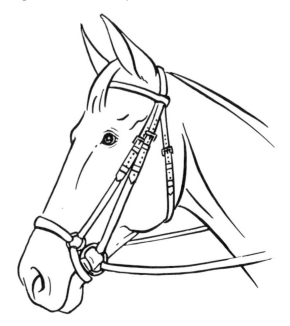

13 A properly tacked-up horse being lunged. It is important to make certain that the saddle is secure before attaching the side reins. Note the position they are fixed to the saddle – as near as possible to the rider's hand position although the hands would in reality be a little above the wither. The horse has boots 'all round' to prevent him from injuring himself which is especially easy to do on a relatively small circle

14 Jenny Loriston-Clarke showing how to train the horse to do lateral work. The rider is doing what is known as 'short rein' work and is quite close to the horse. Long-reining is done more frequently, either with two reins on a circle (one direct to the hand of the trainer, the other on the outside of the horse coming round the hind-quarters); or with the trainer driving the horse between the reins and keeping a few yards behind. This would be normally done with the reins to the bit to teach the horse to accept the bit before it is ridden

use of side reins prior to riding the horse, so that he may develop the right outline, thus making muscle in the correct places, i.e. his crest, back and loins and so making things easier for him when ridden. The length of the side reins should be such that they encourage this muscle build up to take place, do not allow hollowing, nor a fixed low head carriage.

Early Ridden Lessons

The first few weeks of riding the young horse should be concentrated on making him go forwards with some energy, not dragging himself along on his forehand but driving himself from his hindquarters. In conjunction with this, as energy comes forwards to the rider's hands, a contact with the mouth should be taken lightly and then maintained with a hand that invites the horse to accept and yield to the bit. The aim at this stage should be to help the horse find his balance so that he can carry himself and his rider with the least difficulty.

He must learn to negotiate the school, to go round the edge, into the corners, make 20-metre circles and change the rein on a diagonal **(Fig.9)**. He must be able to do this in walk and trot. He can learn to strike off to canter on the correct leg even though it may take him a few days before he can negotiate a complete circuit of the school. At this stage, the rider may encourage the correct lead by beginning in a corner.

It will be essential to the young horse's education that he does sometimes work outside the school, although, for safety's sake, his early lessons should be within it. When he goes out and about he should have learned to be controlled, for his sake and that of others. He must learn to go quietly in company with other horses and to leave them without fuss. He will exper-

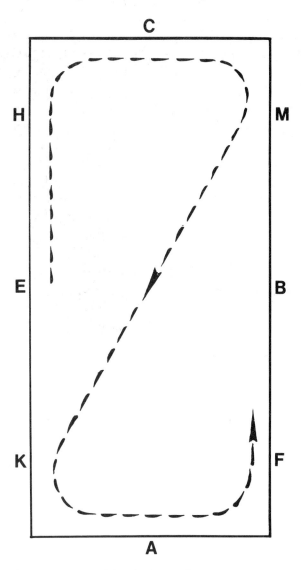

Fig. 9 Change of rein across the diagonal

ience many things, including other animals and traffic, which may at first frighten or puzzle him but which he will overcome through his trust in his rider. He will have to learn about different surfaces and how to handle himself on slippery or deep going, for although many advanced tests at competitions are often on purpose-built arenas, the earlier tests are frequently on poorer going, and I know from experience how invaluable it is to be able to perform whatever the weather can throw at you.

Fig. 10 There are numerous variations on **School figures** – by using the school imaginatively and to its fullest extent, you stretch your horse both physically and mentally – he is more likely to keep working actively and to be listening to you because he will be wondering where he has to go next

Fig. 11 Further school figures

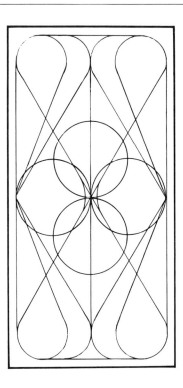
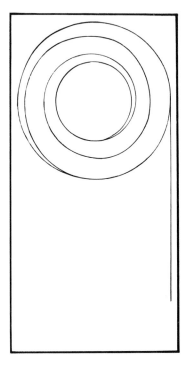

TIPS FOR LUNGEING AND LONG-REINING

- Invest in a few lessons if you are inexperienced.
- Wear boots that will not slip.
- Do not wear spurs as they can cause you to trip.
- Wear gloves in case rein is pulled through hands.
- Fit boots or bandages on horse to protect his legs.
- Ensure cavesson is properly fitted.
- Use a lunge whip.
- Use a proper lunge rein or long reins.
- Ensure side reins, if used, are of the correct length.
- Do not let reins become entangled with your own or the horse's legs.
- Never let the horse go with a trailing rein.
- Do not wrap any round your fingers or hands.

RIDER'S TIP – SCHOOL FIGURES

- Make a point of riding your school figures at home as accurately as possible **(Figs.10–11)**.

- Prepare your horse for each change of direction with a half halt, think ahead, and know where you are going.

- Ride to markers.

8

BASIC PRINCIPLES

In the previous chapter, early acceptance of the aids and obedience to the rider has been discussed. As time goes on, a higher degree of acceptance must be achieved, resulting from systematic training by use of school movements.

Throughout the work and over a period of years, the basic ingredients for success will be the purity of the gaits, straightness, balance, suppleness, rhythm, impulsion, the shape of the horse during his work (outline) and submission (or in better terms, perfect co-operation) from the horse to the rider's will. All this is easier said than done as it is very easy to make mistakes, to turn a collected walk into a pacing walk, a trot into a shuffle by over restriction or a canter into four beats from lack of impulsion. The first and foremost of the rider's aims, after having taught the horse to go forward, to accept a contact and execute simple exercises in the school is to develop and maintain the correct sequence and regularity of steps within each gait (see below). This means that the rider must become aware at once of any irregularities, such as lack of rhythm, loss of rhythm, unevenness of stride, unlevelness or lameness. The horse must learn from his rider the precise speed and rhythm which is required in each gait. These two words, speed and rhythm, cannot be separated as a rhythm cannot

evolve unless a certain speed is maintained. The rider must find a speed at which his horse can maintain an even rhythm. It will not be possible to maintain rhythm without balance, therefore the rider's thoughts must also be directed towards helping his horse to carry himself. Only when the horse is balanced, steady in his rhythm and supple, will he be able to respond to his rider's wishes with ease.

The Gaits

In order to obtain purity of the gaits, rhythm and balance, you must first consider the gaits of your own particular horse and know how to avoid spoiling them, or, in some cases, even improve their quality. Let us first take the walk.

Walk

The walk is a gait of four-time, the sequence of hoof beats being near hind, near fore, off hind, off fore. A horse should walk with purpose and make the four-beat sequence clear to the onlooker. Each foot must be picked up actively and put down firmly and squarely to the ground. Lack of impulsion will prevent this clear picture as the feet then tend to drag, the hind feet sometimes even make a furrow. Too much uncontrolled impulsion can cause imperfection as one or more feet appear to scurry to keep up with the others. This irregularity can manifest itself in unevenly sized steps, un-rhythmic steps, or, worst of all, an incorrect beat with the sequence becoming two instead of four, i.e. two legs on the same side will swing forward simultaneously and the horse paces. This discrepancy, allowed to develop, can be very difficult to correct.

To start with, it is essential that you keep your horse going forward and do not

15 Free walk on a long-rein – here the horse should take his maximum possible stride, lengthening his outline and seeking the bit with the nose in front of the vertical. The horse should be more active than this one appears to be

Fig. 12 Working trot – the pace at which most early school work is carried out

Fig. 13 Collected trot

Fig. 14 Extended trot – note the differences in the horse's outline

allow him to hang behind the leg nor cause him to take steps which are shorter than his natural length stride by restricting him. To learn the natural length of a horse's stride, ride him on a long rein so that he can stretch **(15)**. Then you can feel what he is capable of. When you take up the reins, do not interfere with the stride but try to use the aids so that control is achieved without destroying the natural steps.

Collected Walk

A collected walk will follow much later and only comes from the development of engagement of the hindquarters and greater submission to the aids. However, it must be said here that in a collected walk, the steps will be shorter than the natural steps and the hind feet will not overtrack, but there will be no restriction or loss of the four-beat sequence.

Extended walk will be discussed later on. It is closer to the natural-length stride but, due to increased impulsion, it covers more ground.

Trot

The trot is a two-beat gait, with diagonal pairs of legs working together, i.e. off hind, near fore, and near hind, off fore. Between each pair of diagonal legs touching the ground there should be a moment of suspension during which time the horse can cover ground. This period of suspension may be less in a novice horse but becomes more pronounced with the build up of impulsion **(Figs.12–14)**. It is necessary to acquire a moment of suspension but it can only be maintained through correct rhythm and regularity. It should never lift the horse upwards without taking him forwards as well, otherwise a false trot can evolve, nearer to the passage than a correct trot. With the clear, two beats of the trot, the rider should find it easy to feel for regularity and thus develop a rhythm. It will be important to the horse's suppleness for the rider to change diagonals when training in the rising trot and he should discipline himself to do this **(Fig.15)**.

Collected trot will be discussed later but suffice it to say here that it is vital to have

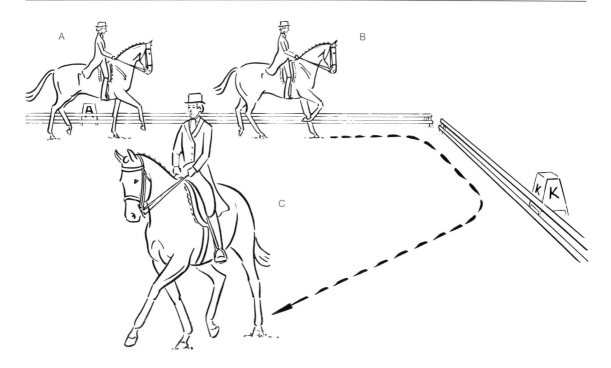

Fig. 15 Lengthening strides in trot – A the horse is approaching in a balanced way. B He is prepared for the turn into the diagonal by the use of a half halt. (At Novice standard this is only to a small degree for the purpose of further engaging the hindquarters and bringing the horse together.) C Once on the diagonal, when the horse is straight, he may be asked to lengthen his stride. The rhythm of the working trot and the lengthened trot must be the same

sufficient impulsion to give a good moment of suspension and never to restrict freedom. Extension in trot evolves from collection and impulsion, but is made more possible if you ensure that in every gait you adhere strictly to the balance and rhythm established for your particular horse.

Canter

The canter is a three-beat gait, the sequence being near hind, near fore and off hind together, off fore (leading leg), or off hind, off fore and near hind together, near fore (leading leg). As with trot, there

is a period of suspension, but this occurs after the three beats have finished and before the next three begin. It is during this moment that a horse effects a 'change in the air', so unless this moment of suspension is correctly developed from the beginning, tremendous problems can occur later. A young horse will not necessarily show this suspension until he learns to balance himself and his rider, which may take some weeks. At first, he will tend to fall onto his forehand, and only development of self carriage through engagement of the hindquarters will help him to reach a state of balance that enables him to define a clear moment between strides.

In due course, a collected canter will follow which from its very nature will even more clearly define the moment of suspension. It is very easy, however, to destroy the correct beat of the canter by losing impulsion or restricting the gait and allowing it to become flat and four beat. If this should happen, it will be disastrous for the future, so immense care must be taken from the outset.

Extensions will also be required to show a clear moment between strides. One of the pitfalls here is that the horse, in his exuberance, may simply want to gallop off, or from uncontrolled impulsion falls onto his forehand, sometimes losing the correct three-beat sequence for four beats.

Balance

The greatest early factor in training is to put the horse in balance. Whatever ingredients you strive for in the gaits or whatever movements you try to teach your horse, none will be effective, unless the horse is balanced and is able to carry both himself and his rider. This self carriage must be implemented by careful preparation through sympathetically and consistently given aids, which include the ability to control speed, being able to keep the horse straight where required and curve him into corners and on circles.

Lack of balance shows itself in a number of ways: the majority of the horse's weight may be on the shoulders (forehand) or on one shoulder more than another; the horse may alter his stride to keep himself on his feet; use his neck and head to save himself either by lowering his head and leaning on his rider's hands or by suddenly throwing it in the air; or his hindfeet may not truly follow the forefeet.

GIVE AND RE-TAKE THE REINS

A very useful exercise to develop self carriage is to 'give and re-take' the reins (Figs.16–17). This does not mean that the reins should suddenly be thrown away, nor suddenly caught up, giving the horse a jerk in the mouth!

The idea is to release the contact either with both reins at the same time or by one rein (usually the inside rein) very gradually for a few strides. The contact will then be gently retrieved and the horse returned to the control between leg and hand.

During this period the horse should remain calmly in balance, in rhythm and in outline.

You can use this exercise in any gait and at any time in the school as a test to discover whether the balance is correct, or to teach the horse that he may not rely on his rider for support but must go under his own steam.

Figs. 16–17   Giving and retaking the reins

Corners and Circles

During the early part of the training, ensure that aids are applied evenly, to make the horse straight and to give the gaits maximum opportunity to remain pure and even. At all times, including on the lunge or during long-reining, the hind legs must follow the track of the forelegs. Often, especially on a stiff side, the hind feet follow a different track from the forefeet. Even young or unbroken horses will have a stiffer side and corrections must continually be made to check that this situation does not become established. Sometimes the cause is too much speed, but lack of balance can also contribute resistance through the back or in the mouth. You must be continually aware of these possibilities and ready to correct the fault.

In conjunction with working evenly forwards, the horse will also be asked to adopt a curve in appropriate places, i.e. corners and circles. These curves will be minor to start with as the horse should neither be asked to go deeply into corners nor to perform less than a 20-metre circle. The vital factor of these curves will be to ensure that they are described evenly from nose to tail; no more bend in the neck than in the body, no tilting of the head instead of correct flexion, the hind legs faithfully tracking the forelegs. The curves will be achieved by firmer use of the rider's inside leg to keep the horse out in conjunction with the outside rein held to the neck (not away from it). The outside leg will be slightly behind the girth, holding the hindquarters in place and the inside rein will be inviting the flexion. This flexion is to encourage the horse to look the way he is going and at this stage is little more than a softening of the horse's mouth to the rider's inside hand. There may be some resistance against the bend from the mouth, poll, neck or back muscles but a persistent yet polite use of the aids gradually should persuade the horse to conform. It will be most important to make sure that the bend (curve) is equal in each direction so that the muscle system is developed evenly.

Transitions

Putting the work together involves changes, known as transitions, from one gait to another. These transitions must necessarily be asked for very carefully, with much preparation, as any suddenness of aids will cause the horse to do several things disastrous to his training; he may throw up his head, open his mouth, put his tongue over the bit, overbend, use his weight in different directions, swing his hindquarters and so on. If the rider is careful, giving the horse plenty of time to comply following the aids, the transition should be accomplished smoothly and without difficulty. The voice may be used in the early stages to aid the procedure. Much concentration should be given to the steps or strides during transitions. Pay strict attention to rhythm and regularity to ensure the evenness and equality of the steps.

Outline

Throughout the preliminary training, you should be very aware of the shape (outline) the horse is attaining through his work. This is of enormous importance – the horse comes to his shape through systematic work and not from any pulling or pushing by the rider to force him. At this stage, the aim will be to put the horse in such a position that he can carry himself and his rider through a series of simple movements in an arena without losing his balance or resisting the aids, maintaining a steady outline. Horses will vary in their outlines due to their conformation but the rider should have a constant picture in his mind of the shape he wants to achieve. One point to consider during this phase is that the aim of training is gradually to transfer weight from the forehand to the hindquarters, so it is never helpful to the horse to allow him, or to put him, on the forehand. From the outset a young horse should learn to use his hindquarters energetically to take him forwards, calmly and straight.

RIDER'S TIP – SITTING TROT

It is not compulsory for the rider to 'sit' in tests until Elementary standard, but of course, preparation should be made in training. The young horse will be worked in rising trot until his physique has built up to carry the weight of his rider. Unless the rider has a secure seat, sitting trot can cause much harm to the horse's back or to the gaits, making them irregular or uneven. It can also cause damage or to the horse's mouth if the reins are used for balance.

9

PROGRESSION: HALF HALT AND LEG YIELD

Progression from phase one to phase two of training is quite demanding and in some cases can make or break the possibilities for the future. Rider and horse are now under some pressure to reach towards the goal of advanced work. The horse now has to learn to engage his hindquarters more, the first step towards real impulsion, he has to accept a greater degree of 'putting together', the introduction to collection, and he has to learn to yield more to his rider's inside leg and allow his forehand to be 'positioned', a preliminary step to shoulder-in.

Preparation

The half halt and shoulder-in are the most valuable exercises in the entire training. To execute them satisfactorily requires all the basic principles, and when mastered, they provide the preparation for every other exercise.

There is a temptation to try to hurry this period and also a danger of making insufficient advance. Because of these difficulties, you need to plan your work carefully on a daily basis, and at the end of each day's training, analyse the position. Problems will arise either from lack of comprehension or for physical reasons. The rider must understand the horse's mental processes. She should realise that

any instruction given to the horse will be memorised. This can work tremendously to the rider's advantage or conversely it can be a disadvantage, if, by mistake, the wrong instruction is given. The horse cannot interpret indistinct instructions, so will inevitably be confused. Only those aids which are repeated clearly for each specific requirement can be obeyed willingly and without problems.

There must also be clear understanding of the horse's physical ability to comply with his rider's wishes. Firstly, the horse cannot respond unless he understands, but even having done so, his thought transference to his muscle system has to take place. This having occurred the muscle system has to operate the limbs. Should there be any undue strain on undeveloped muscles or pain, the process could take even longer.

Although a highly trained horse's response appears immediate, this is only because the union between horse and rider is so tightly bonded from years of concentrated work. It is important to remember that younger horses will need sympathetic understanding by their riders of the time and preparation needed for compliance to every movement asked for.

If the horse is allowed to develop in this way, he will be able to withstand the pressures of more advanced work.

Half Halt

Without the ability to accomplish a correct half halt **(Figs.18–19)**, you will have no means of progressing beyond preliminary work. This exercise is absolutely essential in order to collect the horse and obtain impulsion. Many horses are spoilt unnecessarily because of their rider's lack of ability to give the aids correctly. If one views the half halt as a 'gathering together' with the purpose of bringing the hindquarters more under the horse to enable him to drive himself forward more energetically without losing any balance, one can see that there must be complete acceptance of the aids to achieve this, and that the result should bring both mental and physical processes together to a higher degree.

Figs. 18–19 Half halt in trot – a good rider uses half halts automatically, whenever a change of direction, pace or movement is required, or to rebalance the horse during a movement. In advanced dressage the half halt will be so subtle as to be almost invisible to the onlooker. The rider's legs and back drive the horse into a momentarily restraining hand. It is important to hold the extra impulsion created

The Fédération Equestre Internationale (FEI) definition of the half halt is,

a hardly visible, almost simultaneous co-ordinated action of the seat, the legs and the hand of the rider, with the object of increasing the attention and balance of the horse before the execution of several movements or transitions to lesser and higher paces. In shifting slightly more weight onto the horse's quarters, the engagement of the hind legs and the balance on the haunches are facilitated, for the benefit of the lightness of the forehand and the horse's balance as a whole.

There are two main problems in riding a good half halt. The first is co-ordinating the aids, and the second, recognising whether there has been an adequate answer to them.

Taking the problem of the co-ordination, obviously as a rider improves in his seat and learns the feel from practice, he will gradually know what to look for. During this learning period he will make mistakes, either by using his seat and legs too much, creating strong forward energy which he cannot control, or by tension in the hands causing a restriction of any energy created.

Clearly it is no good unless the brain can co-ordinate his limbs to work in such a way that they complement each other. The seat and legs should be asking the horse to go forwards and must maintain the engagement of the hindquarters and the impulsion during the half halt. The hands should then receive the impulsion and control it to obtain the degree of half halt needed.

Used as preparation for a transition, for example, the degree may be slight. Prior to a lateral exercise where more collection is required, the half halt may be more pronounced.

A swinging back

Recognition of the success of the half halt can only evolve through experience but the rider will need to keep several things in mind. As she applies seat and legs, the horse should, of course, respond by coming forward into the hands. He should not surge forward suddenly, but should feel as though he has grown under the seat of the rider, creating more lift, which will be felt as his back arches. This is caused by greater engagement of the hindquarters, and the horse's back should feel soft and yielding as it moves up and down with the rhythm of the steps. This movement of the back is generally described as a swinging back, and denotes suppleness. The rhythm must be kept exactly and energy maintained. Any drop in impulsion will cause the effectiveness of the half halt to be lost. The rider who is new to the half halt will not know how long to sustain her aids, but if the object is to improve balance, to create more energy or to bring the horse more together, only when the horse has given the required answer are the half halting aids relaxed. In an untrained or young horse, the rider may have to ask for a series of half halts to achieve the desired result. This is even more difficult for the novice rider, as it means that he has to engage his brain rapidly after his initial aid to follow this with the repeated aids correctly co-ordinated. His hands must never prevent the horse from forward momentum so he must direct the correct amount of feel and ease to ensure that this continues. By the nature of the aids the horse may interpret them as something more than they are meant to be and may well try to halt instead of half halt.

Degrees of half halt

It is important to realise that the degree can vary enormously from merely giving a 'steadying' aid to the young horse which is his introduction to the exercise to a 'gathering together' in the next stage and then, lastly, aids for collection. Quite often, novice riders make the mistake of losing the effect of their half halt by riding forwards out of it incorrectly. Two things particularly hinder the effect; one is the loosening or over-lightening of the rein to go forward and the other is an over-impulsed transition which may be too sharp, losing the rhythm and balance of the stride. Logically, if the horse has been asked to come together by a combined effect of the aids for the purpose of collecting him or improving his balance, it is futile to release him from the aids or to drive him out of balance by incorrect or overstrong aids. The co-ordination of aids to accomplish a correct half halt should lead the rider towards the feel of the forward transition, but only if she is sufficiently aware of the fact that it is a transition and should be ridden as such; smoothly, gradually and with regular steps. Any loss of energy (impulsion) will immediately render the exercise meaningless.

Towards Engagement

In order to progress beyond the first stages of training, the rider must ask the horse to become more effective with his hindquarters to increase impulsion and lighten the forehand. This is called engaging the hindquarters. To be able to do this, the horse must learn to half halt so that he is more collected and the balance can be transferred from the forehand, by stages, to the hindquarters. The hind legs of the horse should be asked to work under the hindquarters (not behind them) and if this happens properly the croup will begin to lower and the joints of the hind legs will flex, propelling the horse forwards and

upwards. This engagement requires a novice horse to go forwards more than he goes upwards, but as training progresses, he will be sufficiently strengthened to be able to lift more. The high degree of engagement, combined with collection, enables the advanced horse to perform piaffe and passage, as well as enhancing and making easier all other exercises. Any attempts by the rider to sustain engagement must be tempered with a feel for any undue effort put upon the horse's back or loins, as strain to this area can result in resistance or even irreparable damage. It must be stressed that all exercises must be introduced and used in such a way that the horse is not put under mental or physical pressures which cause him harm or distress.

Another very vital point to remember is to keep the horse round in his outline and never to allow him to become hollow. Any attempt to make the horse half halt or to engage him further in a hollow position will not only be impossible for him but may well cause actual muscular damage.

Impulsion

As the horse becomes accustomed to and accepts the aids for further engagement of the hindquarters, he will be able to provide greater impulsion. Without impulsion, the work is worthless, as with no energy force it is a little like trying to turn on a light switch when you are not connected to the electricity supply. The concept of impulsion can be puzzling to the uninitiated and even a problem to those who are! In order to achieve the training principles which lead towards a higher stage, i.e. transference of weight onto the hindquarters to free the shoulders and lighten the forehand, the impulsion desired is not simply a driving forwards but also lift and cadence (supreme rhythm) of the steps. Control of the degree of impulsion is difficult for rider and horse. The horse can only give the impulsion asked for by his rider, so the rider necessarily must regulate it. If the horse is over impulsed, he will not be able to hold his balance and may well lose his rhythm or lean on the hands of his rider. Similarly, if he is under impulsed, he will not be active enough and the rider will end up doing more work than the horse!

Activity

The reader may find that the words impulsion and activity become intermingled in dressage terminology and wonder what exactly is the difference. To put it as simply as possible, impulsion is as described above whereas activity is really to do with the actual use of the hind legs of the horse. This is in relation to flexibility of the joints and the tempo of the steps. For instance, a slow trot might be described as 'inactive', giving the horse too little lift, without also taking him forward. The hind legs would be making a minimal effort and would need to be exerted more effectively. This could also be described as lack of impulsion, which indeed it would be, but without the hind leg being made more active there could be no impulsion.

Leg Yield

Before beginning the shoulder-in exercise, riders may want to make their horse more aware of their inside leg aids and so may decide to use the leg yield for this purpose **(Figs.20–21)**. The leg yield should not be thought of as an exercise which must be ridden in any particular part of the school, as it simply teaches the horse to yield to increased pressure from the rider's leg placed on the girth and from which he is

THE SCHOOLING WHIP

Creating more activity can be best achieved with the aid of a schooling whip, used in conjunction with the leg aids. A sharp flick, administered behind the rider's leg, across the horse's flank, or onto his thigh encourages the hind leg to be picked up in a more active fashion. Some riders use the schooling whip as a punishment. This is not the right way to train a horse. The whip should always be used to aid the legs if they fail to get a response.

Horses vary very much in their reaction to a whip. Some are frightened, some react easily and others will remain dull to its use unless used effectively. Frightened horses can become accustomed to a whip if the rider introduces its use sensibly.

Sometimes it may be necessary to carry a shorter, jumping whip until the horse learns that it will not hurt him. The rider must be prepared to change the whip from one hand to the other extremely quietly until he can carry it in each hand without upsetting the horse. When the long whip is then brought into use it may be laid across the horse's flank and quietly held there while the rider soothes the horse with his voice. In time it will be possible to use the whip normally.

Dull horses do need waking up and it may be necessary to employ a whip to jerk him into a state of mental awareness. This must not be done as a punishment but as a lesson to teach him that he must react immediately to the leg or the light tap of the whip.

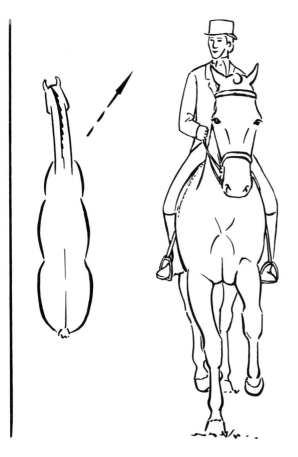

required to move away. The rider may use this to increase the bend, or to lighten the weight of the horse, which may be falling in on a corner or on a circle. He may also use it to increase engagement of the horse's inside hind leg prior to asking him to go forwards with greater impulsion. Initially, the rider may teach the horse by riding on a line parallel to the side of the school and leg yielding into the track. Later, the leg yield can be used in a variety of places **(Figs.22–23)**.

The horse's bend will be very slightly away from the direction in which he is going. In corners or on circles, if the leg yield is used, the bend will remain the same as only a few steps will occur before the corner or circle is resumed.

Fig 20 (Above left) **Leg yield** – the first lateral movement most horses are taught under saddle. The horse is bent slightly away from the direction in which he is moving

Fig. 21 (Above right) **Leg yield** – front view

Figs. 22–23 **Use of the leg yield** – there are many suitable places in school to use leg yield – a useful exercise for the novice horse to teach him to respond to the inside leg of the rider

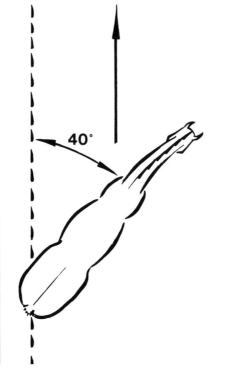

Faults in Outline

Hollowing the horse comes above bit and flattens his back **(Fig.24)**.

Overbending the nose is behind the vertical, evading the bit **(Fig.25)**.

Croup high the horse may be built croup high but he can also use his croup to resist lowering his hindquarters and prevent engagement **(Fig.26)**.

Broken neck when the poll is not the highest point of the neck. Indicates incorrect engagement and evasion of the bit **(Fig.27)**.

Compare these with the correct outline **(Fig.28)**. Here the horse's poll is the highest point of his neck, his nose is on the vertical, and his back is rounded.

Fig. 24 Faults in outline – hollowing

Fig. 25 Faults in outline – overbending

Fig. 26 Faults in outline – croup high

Fig. 27 **Faults in outline** – broken neck

Fig. 28 **Correct outline**

10

SHOULDER-IN AND SUBSEQUENT EXERCISES

Now it is time to teach the horse the next exercise in his training, the shoulder-in. This exercise is so valuable because it gives the rider control over the forehand, which enables him to prepare and position his horse for the various exercises.

Shoulder-in

The FEI definition is as follows:

> The horse is slightly bent round the inside leg of the rider. The horse's inside foreleg passes and crosses in front of the outside leg, the inside leg is placed in front of the outside leg. The horse is looking away from the direction in which he is moving.
>
> Shoulder-in, if performed in the right way, with the horse slightly bent round the inside leg of the rider, and at the correct angle, is not only a suppling movement but also a collecting movement, because the horse at every step must move his inside hind leg underneath his body and place it in front of the outside, which he is unable to do without lowering his inside hip **(Fig.29)**. Shoulder-in is performed 'along the wall' at an angle of about 30 degrees to the direction in which the horse is moving **(Fig.30)**.

Angle of shoulder-in

It must be said that the angle of 30 degrees need not be adhered to strictly. It is more important that the horse shows a balanced way of going with good impulsion and that the quality and regularity of his steps are maintained.

To start with, the angle will be smaller than 30 degrees. One point to remember is that whatever the angle asked for, it should be maintained, otherwise the horse's shoulders will not be under control, the very object of the exercise. Attentiveness to the inside leg aid will be the rider's first criterion, but there must also be an acceptance of the controlling outside hand which is bringing the forehand to the required angle. The outside leg assists the outside hand to maintain angle while the inside hand asks for the flexion. Much can go wrong with the shoulder-in until the co-ordination of aids becomes automatic but beware of bending the horse's neck too much to the inside and beware also of preventing the forward movement by restriction of any kind. Novice horses will only be able to perform a few steps at a time and it could be a while before they can proceed the length of a 40-metre arena. In fact, much damage can be caused by the rider becoming over insistent. The exercise is best taught to the horse in walk as it gives more time for

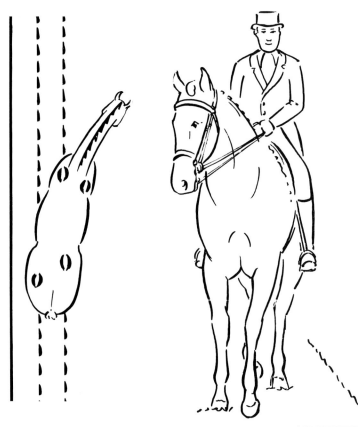

Fig. 29 (Left) **Shoulder-in** – an essential exercise. It is ridden on three tracks, at an angle eventually of 30° to the wall or the centre line, with the horse bent away from the direction in which he is moving. Prepare the horse by establishing the desired bend on a curve, half halt before the turn, maintain the bend then ask for a few strides of shoulder-in before riding away

Fig. 30 **Shoulder-in** – front view.

thought and correction. In a properly angled shoulder-in some collection will be needed and it will be easier for both parties to tackle at a slow gait.

Preparation

In order to achieve the collection, use half halts to engage the hindquarters and create the ability to shorten and heighten the steps. Great care must be taken not to restrict forward movement nor to allow the steps to come out of sequence. During the shoulder-in itself, the rider should help the horse to retain collection by using half halts where necessary. Riders may find it helpful to ride a circle of ten or 12 metres prior to asking for shoulder-in **(Fig.31)**. This gives the opportunity to make the horse more attentive to the aids and to make him well aware of the curve he will be required to give. The movement can also be ridden on a circle **(Fig.32)**.

Straightness

Throughout training, the rider must be very conscious of the straightness of the horse **(Figs.33–35)**. Often the hindquarters come a little too much to the inside, or they swing out on corners or circles. Control of the forehand via the shoulder-in is the best remedy for crookedness as it gives the rider the chance to bring the forehead into a position that the hindquarters must follow. For instance, if the hindquarters are falling in on the long side of the school and the rider takes shoulder-in position, the hindquarters are then more easily kept on the track. This applies in all gaits, although in canter to a lesser degree. Prior to many exercises a slight shoulder-in position can be of enormous help in preparing the horse, helping his balance or engaging his inside hind leg to a greater degree thus making the following exercise easier for him. Exper-

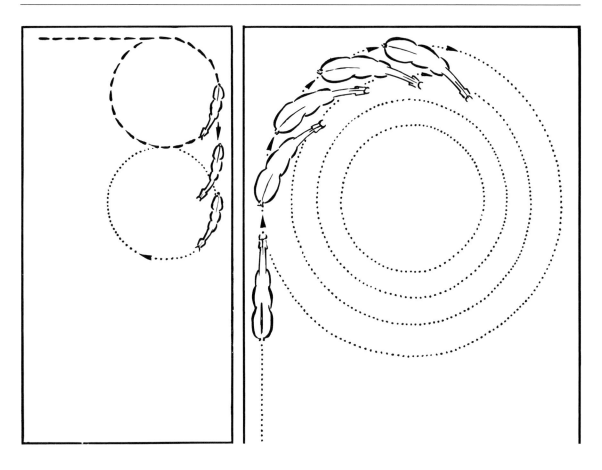

Fig. 31 (Above left) **Preparation for shoulder-in** – a 10-metre circle to establish the bend, before riding down the long side of the arena.

Fig. 32 **Preparation for shoulder-in** – this can be ridden in several parts of the school – along the walls, down the centre line, and on circle

ienced riders will use the shoulder-in aids to some degree much of the time even simply riding round the school, to aid control. This exercise, like all exercises, is not an end in itself but an absolute necessity to correct training **(Figs.33,34,35)**.

The shoulder-in is also invaluable for increasing the horse's suppleness and, used correctly, it will greatly strengthen his back muscles, allowing him to swing under his rider without tension or resistance.

Variations within a Gait

Together with this work must come variation within each gait to supple the horse further. The half halt will have started to contribute towards suppleness and will enable the rider, with his greater control of the forehand, to ask the horse to lengthen or shorten his stride. Before he can satisfactorily lengthen within a gait he must first be collected to some degree otherwise there is a likelihood of lack of engagement and subsequent loss of balance. Any loss of balance may cause irregularity or unlevelness and probably resistance as well.

If the collection and balance are satisfactory, some lengthened steps may be requested, but always bear in mind that absolute regularity and rhythm should be maintained. Most important are the tran-

Fig. 33 **Straightness – correct**. It is one of the basic principles of dressage that the horse should be straight, i.e. its hind feet should follow in the tracks of the forefeet

Fig. 34 **Straightness –** wide behind

Fig. 35 **Straightness –** crooked

Fig. 36 **Halts** – front view. Halts must be square when seen from both the front and side. The horse should on no account step backwards, but should remain motionless yet alert to the rider for the required length of time

Fig. 37 **Halt** – side view

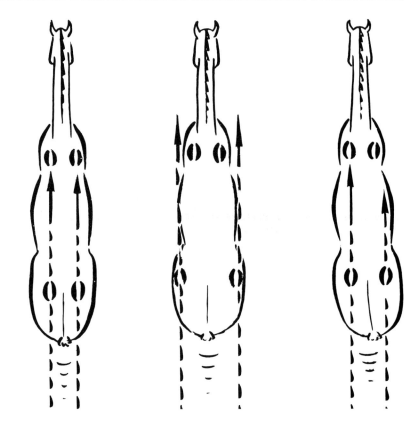

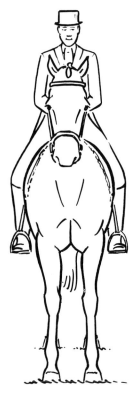

sitions from shortened to lengthened strides and vice versa. The half halt will help to achieve smoothness of these transitions and keep the horse in balance, so that he does not fall onto the forehand or lose engagement of the hindquarters. The amount of lengthening will be governed by the horse's ability to keep his balance and the shortening is dependent upon his acceptance of the aids for collection. A novice horse should only be asked to lengthen for a few strides at first, until systematic work builds up strength in the hindquarters, thus enabling him to give more impulsion.

Halt

Transitions are so vital to the smoothness and ease of a performance that throughout your work, great attention should be given to them. This would include the transitions to and from halt and the halts themselves **(Figs.36–37)**. At first, the novice horse will be required to halt only from walk but as he progresses, direct transitions from the other gaits will also be requested. Similarly, he will be expected to go directly from a halt to a trot or canter. Therefore, it is necessary that during transitions the horse is balanced and that he accepts the aids without resistance. If this is so, he will be able to achieve a balanced 'square' halt on the aids, from which he can easily comply with his rider's next command. Some horses seem to halt squarely quite easily and others appear to find it much more difficult. However, providing that the rider has kept the hindquarters engaged properly and kept his horse 'on the aids' the problem should be minimised. In the event of a crooked halt, the shoulder-in should be used to straighten it or in an un-square halt a schooling whip may be used to bring up the hindquarters while asking for the halt to be maintained. The horse should on no account step backwards, but should remain motionless yet alert to the rider for the required length of time **(16)**.

Rein-back

As work on the halt establishes, the rein-back may also be introduced, but only one or two steps should be attempted at first and only if the horse is accepting the aids so willingly that he can step backwards without resistance **(Figs.38–40)**. Novice riders often try to pull the horse backwards but this can only result in stiffness and possibly damage to the back muscles, and also to the mouth. True engagement of the hindquarters in the halt, balance and an acceptance to the aids will permit the rider to get the horse to rein back without difficulty. If the horse should hollow in any way or overbend, it will be impossible to achieve the exercise to any degree of satisfaction. Someone 'on the ground' can be of help in assisting the rider by tapping the horse's front legs with a schooling whip but the best result comes from having progressed systematically to a stage where the horse can easily respond to the question.

Walk Pirouette

As the horse is now able to be collected to a degree, and understands the half halt and shoulder-in, he is ready to learn the walk pirouette. Ultimately he will be required to execute 180-degree turns but he may learn by performing a turn of 90 degrees or less, depending on the rider's prowess at the exercise. The turn will be best controlled by first obtaining some collection in walk, then by 'positioning' by use of the shoulder-in aids. You then decide where to make the turn and, without

losing the hindquarters to the outside, bring round the forehand. Not only must the hindquarters be strictly controlled, but so must the sequence of walk steps. Any loss of impulsion will result in broken rhythm. It is always better when teaching the horse to make the pirouette larger rather than smaller so that the gait can be maintained, also it will give more time for the rider to think about the aids, paying particular attention to the use of the inside leg to retain the impulsion and the outside rein for containing the gait and bringing the forehand round. The inside rein will be giving the direction and flexion and the outside leg will be preventing any outward tendency of the hindquarters.

Throughout this section of the training, you should have uppermost in your mind the correctness of your horse's gaits, his outline resulting from impulsion and acceptance of the aids and his suppleness, and at all times be aware of your own correct position and influence over your horse.

16 *(Left)* Alan Doxey demonstrates a good square halt. In this exercise the judges would assess whether the halt is straight as well as square and whether there is sustained immobility. Here Alan salutes the judge at the start of a test by taking off and replacing his hat. Women 'salute' by dropping their right hand to her side and giving a slight bow

Figs. 38–40 Rein-back – a movement in two-time

RIDER'S TIP – SPURS

Spurs are compulsory in tests from Medium standard onward, but of course should be introduced much earlier. If a short neck spur is used to begin with, fitted correctly on the rider's boot (many are worn far too low) and used sensibly they can be introduced gradually quite early in the training **(Fig.41)**. They should not be used instead of a correct leg aid. The schooling whip will reinforce the aid. The spur may or may not come into contact with the horse's side, but if it does, it should only give the leg aid the opportunity to be lighter. Spurs should not be used as a punishment, nor continuously, as this will only serve to deaden the horse to the aids. For competitions, spurs may not be worn upside-down and they must be made of metal. However, there is no restriction on the type of shank used, and rowels are permitted providing they are fitted vertically.

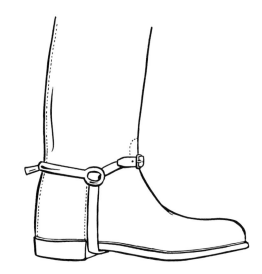

Fig. 41 **Correctly fitted spurs** – worn with the longer side on the outside of the boot, pointing downwards. Take care that they lie on the spur rest of the boot and do not slip down. For competitions, spurs may not be worn upside-down and they must be made of metal, but there is no restriction on the type of shanks, and rowels are permitted providing they are fitted vertically

DIFFICULTIES WITH SHOULDER-IN

Faults

- Not enough angle.

- Not enough bend.

- Bend only in neck.

- Angle not held.

- Losing impulsion.

- Falling back into track.

Solutions

Most faults occur because the rider's aids are not clear or are un-coordinated.

- The correct use of the inside leg, sending impulsion to a controlling outside hand enables the rider to position the forehand to the angle required.
- If the shoulder-in varies it is because impulsion has failed, making it impossible for the rider to maintain it.
- Lack of bend is mainly due to the rider being unaware that he has not requested or not obtained enough.
- Any evasions should be dealt with by riding forwards onto a circle in order to correct impulsion and bend.
- Collection, or lack of it, is often a cause of difficulty and even more often, restriction, which is mistaken for collection.

11
RE-TRAINING THE OLDER HORSE

Re-training older or spoilt horses can be a tremendous problem but is a challenge which can also be irresistible to those interested. One of the first problems is that such horses find it difficult or even impossible to put their trust in anyone. They may have been ill-treated intentionally or from ignorance in the stable or when being ridden. Their response to aids may be very poor, either because they have not really been trained at all or because they have been badly ridden, their mouths are unresponsive and so are their sides!

Attitude

Their attitude may well be a big problem too as they may have learned how to resist their rider's wishes in a variety of ways. They may have learned to intimidate their owner in the stable by biting or kicking, or napping when being ridden. The owner must first try to gain trust by becoming the horse's friend on the ground and then not ruining the relationship when mounted! It does not follow, however, that because a horse is unwilling to do what you want when being ridden he is also unpleasant in the stable (17). On the contrary, some of the nappiest horses I have known have been as nice as pie in the loose box! It can be pretty upsetting to find that the horse

whose confidence you thought you had won has a sudden fit of 'whipping round' at some indiscernible object, or standing on end when simply asked to trot round the school and nothing you can do apparently has any effect. It is also frightening and can be dangerous unless some form of control is established. Reform has to take place. A psychological approach can only succeed to an extent in that any understanding by the rider of why the horse might be doing something is a help. He cannot unfortunately rationalize with his equine friend nor discover exactly what was the origin of his problem. Only by being prepared to take an immense amount of time and patience can he hope to succeed.

First Steps Forwards

The first task is to persuade the horse to go forwards when he is told. He may be oblivious to any leg aid, so the use of a schooling whip to make him understand may be essential. However, some horses learn to shut off from its use, having been beaten in the past. This is one of the greatest problems a rider can encounter as it can, on rare occasions, be insurmountable. Even a spur used in such cases has no effect. Nevertheless, it is to be hoped that by repetition, the horse will learn to respond, and from reward will begin to respond positively. If he does so, he will gradually learn to work 'forwards' mentally and physically and, as a result, all his muscles which have hitherto been stiffened by misuse or little use, will now begin to relax. As they do, his attitude may improve as he finds the work easier but sometimes stiff muscles are painful and their use could cause a different reaction. Resistance is frequently attributed to a horse's mental state – riders often say 'my horse does not *want* to do this exercise' but the cause is just as likely to be because he *cannot* do what is asked. Painful muscles can actually prevent the horse from doing what the rider wishes and the resistance is only in that it is not possible.

Don't Resort to Short Cuts!

It would seem that to make the horse more supple would be next on the agenda, but with re-training, another component that needs to be tackled urgently is the acceptance of the bit. No amount of getting the horse to go forward will be of any benefit unless he also responds to the hands. Many riders at this point fail as patience gives way and they look for the short cut. To make a horse yield to the hands can be done in many ways: with the use of stronger bits, martingales or draw reins to mention a few, and these methods do have the effect of giving some control and making the horse lower his head to a manageable position. They may work for a particular rider but if the horse is passed on unless the same method is used he will be just as uncontrollable. In any event, there are stipulations in the rules for dressage that they may not be used in competition, so for our purposes they are useless. Unless the horse is taught the correct acceptance of leg and hand and

learns to respond in a snaffle bridle he will be no use for dressage. Different bits or other items of saddlery will only prolong finding the ultimate answer.

Flexions

If the horse is to learn to go properly in a snaffle, he must first go forwards, but then in order to loosen those areas which have become resistant, the rider should tactfully teach his horse to flex, first at the poll and as this begins to relax, then flex the jaw.

Flexions can only be successful if the rider has a sympathetic approach and good co-ordination between hands and legs. Pulling a particular rein in order to get the horse to flex may only make him more resistant. The object will be to be able to get the horse to very slightly turn his head (not his neck) to each side at the rider's wish without being dead in the mouth **(Fig.42)**. As the rein is taken to the required side, the rider must judge its success by assessing whether the horse has 'given' where the head joins the neck as the pressure is applied and whether the mouth on that side feels hard or softer. It may be necessary to repeat the same flexion several times or to take the opposite flexion and achieve some result from that. One flexion is almost certain to be more difficult than the other. Although this will probably need more work on it, do not become obsessed as eventually the horse must become equal and work on both sides will help to achieve this object. Vertical flexions are also employed to accustom the horse to the snaffle **(Fig.43)**. The rider should feel some softening in the mouth as the flexions are taken and should also feel some movement of the bit in the horse's mouth as his lower jaw yields. If no movement of the bit happens from the use of the flexions it may be necessary for the

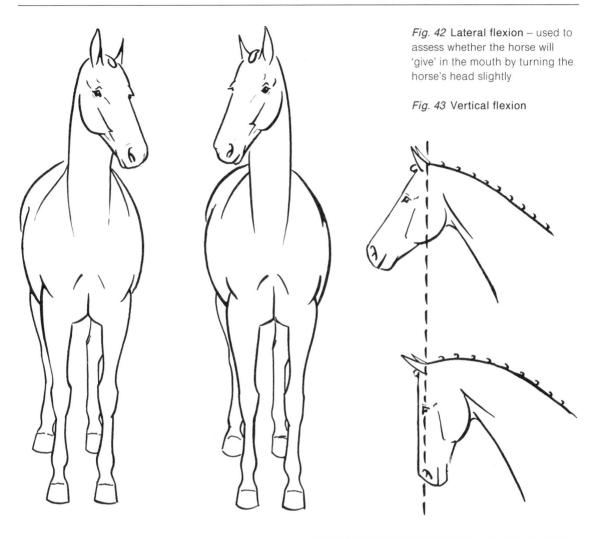

Fig. 42 Lateral flexion – used to assess whether the horse will 'give' in the mouth by turning the horse's head slightly

Fig. 43 Vertical flexion

rider to make this occur by some alternate action of the hands. All action by the hands should be a feel and ease motion done by the fingers rather than by a shut hand. In fact, the method will only work if the rider has the ability to use his fingers effectively. Any rigidity or 'setting' by the hands may only exacerbate the resistance.

In the case of established resistance by the mouth, some work done on the lunge on side-reins can be a help but only if the person lungeing is capable of driving the horse to the bit from behind and only if the length of the side rein permits a correct head carriage. Some spoilt horses will lean on the side-reins and a more satisfactory answer does come from ridden work.

Patience Pays

When the horse has learned to answer the aids, which may take several months, the rider can continue with his normal training programme. In the case of 'nappy' horses there can be continual stumbling blocks, as every time the work becomes more demanding, the horse will recall whatever trick he has learned in the past and use it to evade the aids. Napping takes many forms but generally, any avoidance of the bit or the rider's legs can be classed as such. The only answer is that the horse must learn to obey the aids. Systematic training via the school exercises will gradually form the horse to the rider's wishes as he becomes physically able to comply with them. Suppleness will ease the difficulties of the movements for him and allow him to find freedom of the gaits, which has hitherto been impossible. As the work becomes easier, clearly the horse's mental attitude will improve and so the whole situation can alter.

As I have said, patience is the keyword to re-training. Some people will find it fascinating and others a bore. If the latter, it may be best left to someone else, as frustration will only cause exhaustion and irritation and get you nowhere.

Many people will be of the opinion that older horses cannot be re-trained. This is not the case. Horses are far cleverer at learning in old age than we are and can go on changing and improving until retirement!

17 (Opposite) Owners should try to gain trust by becoming the horse's friend in the stable

Part 3
INTERMEDIATE WORK

12
TOWARDS COLLECTION . . . AND EXTENSION

As training progresses and the basics become established in the horse's mind, further physical development must take place to bring the horse to a stage where he can take more weight onto his hindquarters. Work in the school will gradually bring about this change. The horse will now be able to become more collected.

Collection

Correct collection is of utmost importance and is often very difficult to attain. Providing you keep uppermost in your mind that the motivation of the hindquarters is the first criterion and only then may you gather the horse together more by the use of half halts, you will not go too far wrong. The gathering together must never interfere with the forward impulse and the horse must be given the freedom to comply by sympathetic use of your hands. In collection, there should be a shortening and heightening of the steps in walk, and a greater moment of suspension in trot and canter. If impulsion has been maintained, the horse will still cover ground even in these movements; if he does not, the collection will be incorrect.

There is much talk about the size of the steps in collection in relation to other gait variations such as medium or extended work, but beware of being too pernickety about this point, as it has hidden dangers which can destroy the natural gaits. The important thing is that the rider observes the basic principles to produce collection, that the difference between collected paces and medium and extended ones are obvious to the onlooker, and that the correct qualities of the gaits are preserved at all times.

Lengthening

With the horse more collected, all transitions should now become more pronounced. Therefore, the rider can show clearly the start and finish of any particular exercise, which helps to make his test more precise and accurate. He will also be able to produce a better form of lengthening leading to medium and extended paces (18a, 18b). The hindquarters, being more under the horse and able to propel him energetically forward in a balanced way, will allow the horse a freedom of the shoulder, which in turn permits more scope, enabling him to extend.

Maintaining balance and rhythm will be most important, as will the correctness of the transitions before and after any variation. The horse must only give what he is asked, as if he is too impetuous, the regularity of his stride will suffer, so a gradual build up is very important.

The rider should now use collecting and lengthening to increase suppleness but of course both should be used sensibly, with no over-emphasis on either and all basic qualities maintained. Special attention should be given to ensuring that balance is correct and that the horse does not try to use the rider's hands for support but at all times carries himself.

18a This pony shows an active trot with a good bend

18b A Welsh Cob showing an excellent active trot, the activity being shown by the lift from the ground and the reach of the off hind, which is clearly coming into the footprint of the off fore. Another point worth noting is the equality of distance between the two fore legs and the two hind legs

Using Circles

Now that there is an element of collection, smaller circles and half circles can be used to advantage for increasing the bend and the use of the inside hind leg **(Fig.44)**. They may be done in various positions in the school and may vary in size down to ten metres. Ensure that the horse's hind feet follow the track of the forefeet as circles are made smaller so that he is on a correct curve. You may find that the shoulder-in positioning used before and, to a lesser degree, during the circle will help. This can be executed at all gaits.

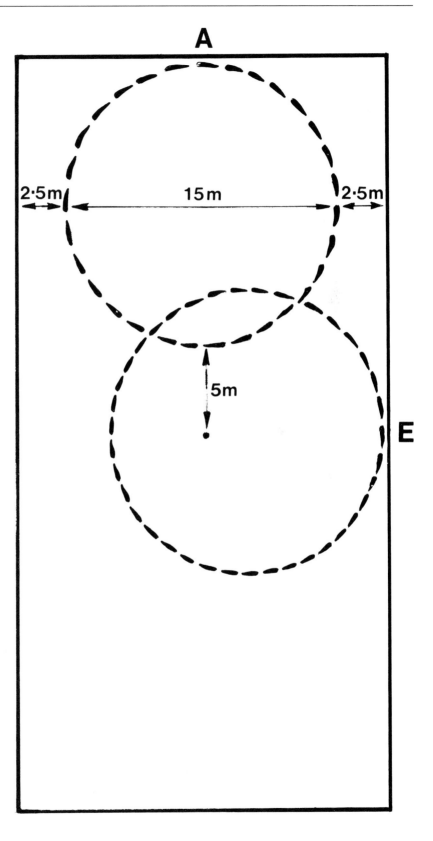

Fig. 44 15m circles – in a 40 × 20m arena at A and E

Introducing Piaffe

It may not be too soon to use the beginning of piaffe (see page 123) to help in engaging the hindquarters to increase collection **(Fig.45)**. The steps should be as collected as the rider can achieve through half halts without interfering with the rhythm of the steps or the forward inclination. Also the horse must remain straight and calm, as to lose either of these factors will defeat any proper engagement, and may also cause upset and resistance. A very gradual introduction should provide some steps useful to the development of collection. Only ask for one or two steps to begin with and never lose sight of the need to go forward immediately if desired. Any halting of the impulsion or dropping behind the rider's leg must be dealt with at once by riding forward energetically.

Fig. 45 Introducing piaffe from walk – The horse is brought to a very collected walk by the use of half halt. If he is 'round' and free from resistance, a transition to short trot is asked for a few strides

RIDER'S TIP – LENGTHENED STRIDES

The horse should be prepared by ensuring he is in balance, well engaged, impulsive and straight.

Only then should you ask for lengthening, which must be kept in the rhythm of the foregoing pace, paying great attention to regularity.

13
LATERAL WORK

Now that some collection is available to the rider, the all-important suppling must take a firm step forward by the introduction and use of lateral exercises. The shoulder-in has already been mentioned but should now be developed both in angle and impulsion. Greater collection and the use of the half halt will make this possible. The leg yield will have been a preparation for lateral work in that it teaches the horse more about the aids and how to use himself in a forwards and sideways way.

Preparation

When beginning any lateral exercise, the rider should ask for only a few steps at a time and because the co-ordination of the aids is difficult for the less experienced rider, it may be advisable to start in walk. This gives more time for the rider to work out what he is trying to do, to make adjustments to the position of the horse and to establish collection, without which the exercise is impossible. More novice riders may put too much emphasis on the sideways part of the exercise whereas in fact the horse cannot travel sideways unless he travels forwards energetically.

Any loss of impulsion halts the exercise, which becomes valueless. Riders should accept less bend to start with and a small angle so that this forwardness is made

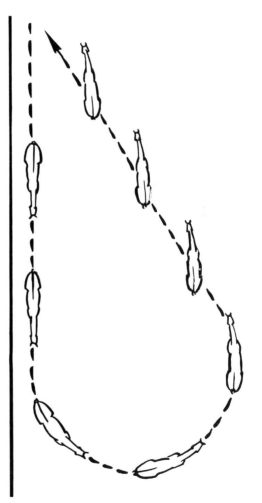

Fig. 46 Approaching the half pass (to the left) – A good way to approach the half pass is to prepare by riding a half volte, which will ensure that the horse already has the correct bend. Half halt before the corner and before moving out of the volte

easier for the horse. It is first of all important to decide exactly which marker to aim for and then to ride for it whether the horse is apparently going sideways or not (**Fig.46**). The flexion can then be kept quite easily. The puzzling 'bend' evolves from the rider's ability to put the hindquarters round their inside leg while maintaining the direction of the forehand. There is sometimes a tendency to curve the horse's neck in mistake for bend without bringing the shoulders properly into position. If the shoulder-in has been used correctly as a preparation, this is less likely to occur. The shoulder-in aids used briefly should help the rider to make a correction to the half pass if required. This is normally done when something goes wrong with the impulsion, bend or collection and gives the rider the chance to re-position.

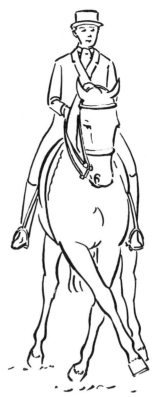

19a Half-pass – this horse is in an excellent position: note the bend of the horse and the correct position of the rider's legs

Fig. 47 Half pass (to the left) – movement of the legs. The weight of the rider is moved to the inner seatbone. The inside leg in on the girth, the outside leg behind the girth

Fig. 48 (Below) Half pass (to the left) – The horse, slightly bent around the inside leg of the rider, should be almost parallel with the long side of the arena. The forehand should be slightly in advance of the quarters

Half Pass

The half pass, which may be the next stage, is ridden on the diagonal in the school (**19**). The FEI definition of half pass is as follows:

> The horse, slightly bent round the inside leg of the rider, should be as close as possible parallel to the long side of the arena, although the forehand should be slightly in advance of the quarters. The outside legs pass and cross in front of the inside legs (**Fig.47**). The horse is looking in the direction of which he is moving.

The bend of the half pass differs from the leg yield and is more difficult for the horse (**Fig.48**). However, the object is to give more freedom and mobility to the shoulders and because the exercise demands more suppleness, the outcome should be greater ease of movement.

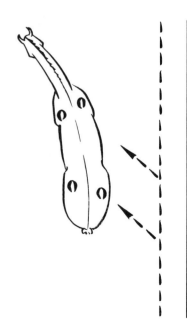

Travers

The travers **(Figs.49–50)** may be taught before the half pass on the diagonal. It is the same exercise but is performed along the wall or on the centre line at an angle of 30 degrees to the direction in which the horse is moving.

Some riders will find that the wall or side of the school helps them control the bend and maintain angle, making the exercise easier than the half pass on the diagonal where there is no distinct line to follow.

19b Travers – head to wall performed by Lucy Farrer on Giovani. The position and effect of the rider's inside leg is evident and the horse looks supple and calm

Fig. 49 **Travers** – quarters in, head to the wall, usually ridden in walk and trot but can be ridden in canter

Fig. 50 **Travers** – front view

Renvers

The renvers **(Figs.51–52)** is the inverse movement to the travers, with the tail instead of the head to the wall. It is more difficult to initiate as the bend has to be altered after the corner and prior to the beginning of the exercise but because of this, it is beneficial to suppleness. Riders may prefer to establish the travers and/or half pass before tackling this exercise **(Fig.53)**.

Fig. 51 Renvers – quarters out, tail to the wall, can be ridden in all three gaits

Fig. 52 Renvers – a more demanding movement for the horse than travers. He is bent to the outside, looking towards the direction of movement

19c Renvers – tail to wall. A good picture demonstrating the bend and the off hind is clearly seen following in the track of the near fore which is correct. The rider is holding a good angle

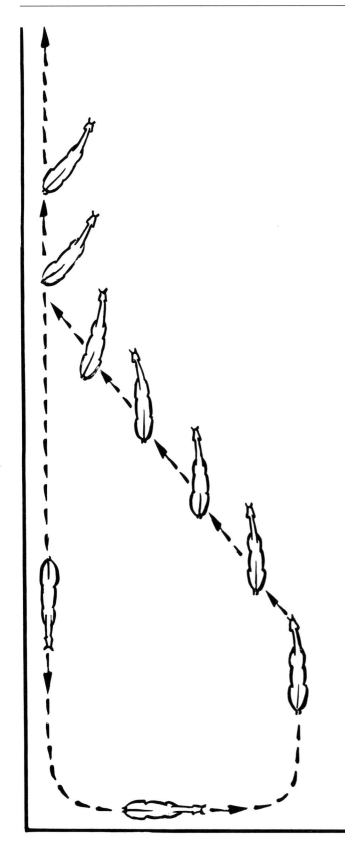

Fig. 53 Half pass followed by renvers

Counter Change of Hand

All this work may take weeks or months, depending upon understanding and ability but only when the horse has fully taken in the requirements should he be asked to begin a counter change of hand. This is merely the riding of a half pass in one direction and at a given marker changing to the other direction. Clearly, if one thinks about it, for the horse there can be a confusion when he has to change his bend and answer a new set of aids in a short space of time. Therefore in the beginning, the wise rider will allow plenty of time for this to take place by riding forwards for a couple of steps or more while re-positioning (via shoulder-in) for the new direction. Eventually, the time span between the two directions will reduce and the horse will be able to change fluently from one to the other. In the case of any difficulty with these exercises or in fact with any other, always go back to walk, diminish the severity of the exercise and start again.

All the lateral exercises may be executed in walk or trot. In canter the horse cannot physically leg yield nor shoulder-in to the degree that he can in trot although shoulder-in position is a reduced form of the exercise and much used for straightening the canter. At this stage, of the horse's training the counter-change of hand in canter is not possible as in order to effect a change of direction it is necessary to use a change of leg in the air (see page 99).

14

COUNTER CANTER

As the lateral work progresses, the horse's physique begins to take on a new look as he becomes supple and lithe, flowing with greater ease from one movement to another. Muscles have now developed showing clearly along the crest, down his back and over his loins to his hindquarters. They also stand out in front of the saddle and on his thighs. The greater strength of his entire body enables him to hold his balance and impulsion better through the movements and to show greater differences within the gaits.

Direct Transitions

The shoulder-in in trot is now well established and can be used to a lesser degree in canter to 'position' the horse prior to half passes, or to keep him straight in transitions. Direct, rather than progressive, transitions are now required of him; that is to say, halt to trot, canter to walk, walk to canter, canter to halt and so on. These transitions can be effected only if there is good engagement of the hindquarters and good collection. In the canter to walk and more especially to halt, there must be a high degree of submission to increased aids as the rider necessarily puts the horse more together and then asks for the downward transition. Often resistance to the

rider's hands causes mouth problems or tensions right through the body. Avoidance to the leg aids can result in the hindquarters swinging about. As you search for 'collection plus' through half halts, you must also attend to the horse's straightness if the transition is to be successful. A small degree of shoulder-in position will give you the power to control the whole length of the horse and be able to adjust any faults immediately. Great care should be taken not to overdo the angle of the canter 'positioning', as if this happens, it can seriously damage the result. Not only will it probably cause resistance, but can also affect the purity of the gait.

Counter Canter

You will now want to work on the counter lead in canter. Some trainers may start it rather earlier, but as with any exercise, there is no hard and fast rule: the ability and temperament of individual horses and the rider's experience must be deciding factors. In fact, it is important not to become stuck in a rut with any of the work or to feel that a new exercise cannot be introduced because 'in the book' it states that A comes before B. Training horses is not like that. It is all a question of feeling

Fig. 54 Counter canter – one of the easiest ways to start teaching this is to introduce a very shallow loop off true lead down the long side of the arena

Fig. 55 Counter canter – adopt the shoulder-in position before asking for counter canter

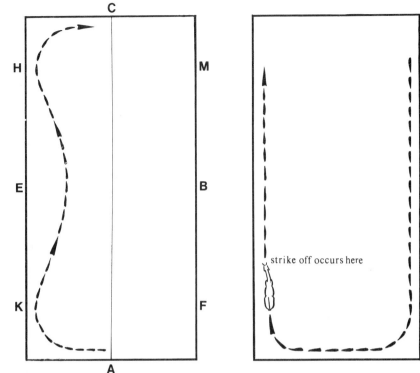

strike off occurs here

when the time is right. Sometimes one exercise will help to improve another, so riders should develop their own judgment.

Work on counter canter will be made a good deal simpler by using the shoulder-in position and maintaining it even if it feels awkward, which can be the case at first. The horse will feel awkward himself and his inclination will be to change legs to balance himself. Clear aids from his rider with the outside leg held back a little more firmly than usual will help him, together with the use of shallow loops, until he understands **(Fig.54)**. Beware of beginning any counter canter exercise too sharply. The horse will need time to adjust his balance, so he will need a gradual approach and good collection. If he is too strung out or in any way on his forehand, the exercise will be a disaster. Once the horse has a full understanding of shallow or gradual curves, he may be asked to strike off to canter on a long side of the school. If so, he will need room to adopt his shoulder-in position **(Fig.55)**, in which case the rider may be wise to take a line parallel to but slightly away from the side, and even then it is best to give an extra clear aid.

As the horse becomes established in this exercise, supple, balanced and obedient, the time has come to move on to the next stage, the 'flying change' or 'in the air' in canter.

RIDER'S TIPS – COUNTER CANTER

- Keep weight to leading leg
- Keep outside leg back
- Maintain canter with inside leg
- Do not lose bend to leading leg
- Despite keeping bend, do not restrict gait with inside rein
- Do not alter direction suddenly

15

FLYING CHANGES

As already said in the previous chapter, you may have chosen to train your horse in a different sequence from the one I am suggesting here, and could have decided to teach the 'changes' in canter before establishing the counter canter. Whether this is advisable or not is up to the individual. Some will argue that once the horse knows the counter canter well, he will refuse to change leg. This is possible and certainly could be a valid argument. It is for each of us to ensure that we strengthen the basic principles at all times and use our powers of feel and common sense to pursue the route ahead. It is up to the rider to make his intention clear to the horse.

Moment of Suspension

To achieve the 'flying change' or 'change in the air' **(20)**, the horse will need to attain a clear moment of suspension between strides. This will result from good collection and impulsion, and it is during this moment that the 'change' occurs. At first, horses often change 'late behind', one hind leg not following through or more rarely, late in front when the inverse situation occurs. These faults may be due to a slow response to an aid or can be because the horse tries to dive onto his forehand. Sometimes, perhaps most commonly, he humps his back, causing a 'lift' of the hindquarters. The horse should be corrected by better control, with attention to his balance and straightness of the gait. Any swinging of the hindquarters or deviation from the intended line will result in poor quality changes.

The Flying Change

Providing your horse has been taught to strike off 'on the aids' immediately and is very obedient to them, if you reverse them, the horse may understand and perform the change without fuss. Having given the change aid, you may continue the canter if the horse fails to answer and repeat the aid with the use of the schooling whip. You may also put the horse in a position in the school where it will encourage him to change leg, i.e. across the diagonal approaching a corner **(Fig.56)**. Sometimes changing from counter lead to true lead is helpful. Whichever way is chosen, if the

20 Flying change – Margitt Otto-Crepin on Corlandus showing the aid for the change-in-the-air from near fore leading to off fore leading. This picture shows that the rider has positioned her outside (left) leg to direct the horse to change its leading leg, which will occur in the moment of suspension which follows the current stride

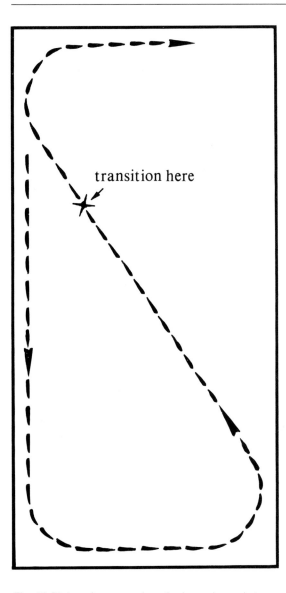

transition here

Fig. 56 Flying change – when the horse is ready to start to learn the flying change, he can be ridden in canter across the diagonal of the school. Aids for the change of legs are given as the horse approaches the change of rein in the corner. This invites him to execute a flying change onto true lead, which he will normally want to do because it is more comfortable for him

horse becomes confused or upset, it is essential to calm him before trying again as many horses' changes are spoilt by impatience on the part of the rider.

Once the horse has learned to make a change in the air, the door is open for a host of new exciting work.

Help from an assistant on the ground to tell you if the changes are right may be a good plan. It can take weeks or months to establish a good 'change' but work towards a good answer at this stage will provide a secure basis for the tempi-changes, which are to come.

Rein-back

Some more work should now be concentrated on the rein-back, which if it began satisfactorily, should not present a problem. The horse will understand the aids and the deportment he must hold. Now it is time to be more precise – an exact number of steps, an immediate response to a forward aid possibly followed by more steps back. The rein-back should be in two-time sequence. The acceptance of the aids, together with good balance, enables the horse to respond correctly. Be careful not to allow your horse to become hollow: this makes the exercise very difficult for him, may cause resistance in his back and his hind feet to drag.

See-saw

Throughout the steps back and during a see-saw (back, forwards, back) the rider's legs should be used to keep the horse straight and on the aids while the hands gently control each step. The steps should be equal in size, not too short nor very long. If the steps are short, it may be because there is tension and the exercise will tend to shuffle. Relaxation allows the horse to step more generously. Long steps can be because the horse is not collected enough and the effort of trying to make such steps can cause the movement to look very unattractive and laboured. If the horse maintains a rounded outline, remaining calmly on the aids each diagonal pair of feet will be lifted and put down in a precise and deliberate manner. Transitions from rein-back to walk, trot or canter should be made only if the balance is right and should be kept straight. A shoulder-in position before the strike-off to canter prevents possible crookedness but to the other two gaits the horse should move forwards from evenly given aids.

Test Practice

At this stage of the training, practice of a specific test may be necessary to discover whether it will come together satisfactorily. Flaws in the training will quickly show up, particularly in connecting one movement to another. Also obtaining sufficient collection or extension at specific points may need some work. Too much practice done on the test as a whole is a mistake but putting several movements into sequence is extremely beneficial.

PROBLEMS WITH REIN-BACK

Fault

If the horse is not fully submissive in his poll and mouth, the rein-back may be hesitant or even jerky and tense, making the steps appear brittle and possibly also uneven.

Solution

To give your horse the best chance of performing this exercise well, maintain the engagement of the hindquarters, keeping the horse forward to your hands. Make sure that the poll is the highest point of the forehand and that both the poll and the lower jaw remain relaxed. With application of light aids, the horse can be expected to come back.

16

EXTENSIONS, CANTER HALF-PIROUETTE

Up until now, so far as medium or extended work is concerned, the gaits have been in a stage of development. The horse has been gradually brought to a stage of impulsion where he can, if asked, extend in balance and rhythm. At first he is asked only for short distances, which are gradually increased until he can hold the longer strides for a complete diagonal or long side of the school. If the collection has been fully understood, the horse will carry more weight on his hindquarters and his shoulders will be lighter and more free. This gives the shoulders more mobility and scope to take a bigger stride, which can cover more ground.

The impulsion will, of course, have to be greatly controlled, in order to show the difference between medium and extended work. This in itself poses problems for the rider who is anxious to get as much as he can from his horse while not allowing over-balancing. It is easy for the horse to get out of hand by over-impulsive action or conversely for the rider to restrict the movement of the horse by using the reins too much. If the horse responds over eagerly to the aids, he may quickly lose rhythm or take uneven steps in his enthusiasm. This is why it is so important to build up gradually so that you have exact control over the size of stride. Use half halts to ensure that you obtain and keep the desired stride. This means that not only should you be able to hold the horse to a medium stride but also have him so attentive to the aids that a slight increase of leg will instantly take him forward to extension.

The Rider's Balance

Because of the enormous energy flowing through the horse in extension, in trot especially there can be a tendency for the rider to balance himself by the reins. Obviously this will only hinder the horse and can very easily cause uneven steps. It is important for both parties to be able to hold their own balance and for riders to be able to maintain a good position. It can be difficult to 'sit deep' in extended trot and not be thrown about, but riders must develop their security in the saddle to achieve this. Generally speaking, the more supple the horse, the easier it is to sit into him. Any rigidity in the back will have an adverse effect. Similarly, this could also be said of the rider!

21 The rider is attempting an extended walk but the horse appears to have fallen a little onto its fore-hand diminishing the freedom and length of stride that should have occured. Also, if the horse had been more forward the stretching of the neck could have been better

Extended Walk

The extended walk should cover as much ground as possible, but must not be hurried or lose rhythm, the hind feet overtracking. Allow the horse to stretch his head and neck, but keep contact with the mouth. In all extensions, the frame of the horse should lengthen a little and the rider should allow the nose of the horse to come in front of the vertical **(21)**.

The difference between extension and medium work is slight. Medium work shows the same qualities but to a lesser extent and on a reduced stride. When performing working, medium and extended work, the rider should aim to show the maximum difference that his particular horse is able to produce.

Canter Half-pirouette

By now, the horse will be fully conversant with the half-pirouette in walk. His collected canter will be established and he will be able to accept a shoulder-in position. Work towards the canter half-pirouette is a natural progression.

Preparation

As with all training, there are various methods of obtaining the desired result and no successful method can be said to be wrong. However, for the less experienced rider, the easiest method may be to learn on a 20-metre circle **(Fig.57)**. The circle will give the rider the chance to make the collection satisfactory, to obtain the bend and to 'position' the horse ready for the pirouette aids. When he feels he is ready, he may try to bring the horse from the 20-metre circle to a ten-metre circle, making sure that the collection, bend and position are still satisfactory. He should then aim to bring the forehand round the hind-

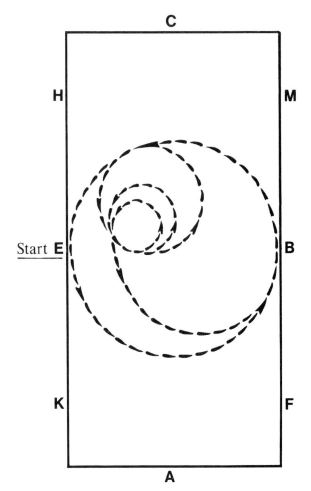

Fig. 57 Pirouette preparation – in the canter half pirouette, the approach and departure must be accurate, providing the foundations for the full pirouette

quarters for two or three strides, using the same aids as for the walk half-pirouette.

Because impulsion is required to keep the canter sequence correct, the rider's inside leg must take this responsibility, while the outside rein brings the forehand round and maintains collection. The outside leg is 'holding' the quarters while the inside rein is giving direction and keeping the flexion. Throughout the exercise the shoulder-in position is used to control the forehand. The rider should aim to execute only the number of strides which he can satisfactorily control while maintaining the correctness of the canter. This may literally be two or three strides, before going forwards out of the pirouette to pick up impulsion, re-establish 'position', bend or correct collection. Do not aim to achieve a complete half-pirouette for some time and only if control is really satisfactory.

Half-pirouette on the diagonal

When your horse has understood the exercise, you will want to make a half-pirouette on a diagonal. Choose your line of approach and use shoulder-in position for control. At your chosen point, give your aid. The horse's first few attempts may not bring him back to the original line of approach, but this line must be regained as soon as possible if the half-pirouette is to be correct.

As with any of these exercises, if there is any confusion or anxiety, go back to basics and review the situation.

PROBLEMS WITH PIROUETTE

All strides should have a forward inclination. Any loss of impulsion, unnatural 'lifting' of the forehand or rushing, should be checked instantly by riding forward onto a bigger circle to re-establish the basic points.

Some horses try to change leg during a pirouette but if they are controlled calmly, this should not happen. As the hindquarters are required to lower during half-pirouettes, any attempt by the horse to hump his back or buck should be dealt with by riding forwards. In this instance, it is likely that there is resistance to the aids for collection so this should be checked thoroughly before trying again.

17

TEMPI CHANGES

When the individual changes in the air in canter have become thoroughly established and are of equal quality on both reins, you may start to think about the next step, i.e. the tempi changes or sequence changes at every fourth, third, second and each stride **(Fig.58)**.

The first stage is a change from one leg to the other followed by another change after a predetermined number of strides. Everything will depend upon the calmness of your horse and his attention to the aids. Any over-excitement may cause the change to be faulty or the horse may simply not react to the aids properly. If he remains straight, calm and balanced he should not find a sequence difficult but, of course, the wise rider will go about the whole matter very gradually.

Concentrate on the Gait

Although obtaining a sequence may be uppermost in the rider's mind, he should always first concentrate on the gait and make certain that it is correct at all times. Imperfections creep in so easily if the horse alters his balance or swings either his forehand or his hindquarters in his effort to effect the change. He may also try to deviate from the original line or refuse to change at all if he is not entirely clear

about the aids. Some horses will try to buck or dash off while they are learning and in these instances only a calm attitude by the rider and a repetition of the situation will help. Occasionally, if the horse becomes too tense, it may be necessary to accept that he may not be ready for sequence changes and will need more time before trying again.

Restrict your work at this point to a change four or five strides following the first one, until that is absolutely clear in the horse's mind. This procedure may be followed until the horse's calmness allows the distance between the changes to be shortened. A particular sequence, such as four-tempi, should be established in the minds of both horse and rider before reducing the number of strides between changes. Some riders find it very difficult to count the strides correctly or to give the aids at the right moment. Unless the horse will allow himself to be 'positioned', that is to say controlled by the shoulder-in aids so that the bend is true for each change, whatever moment the rider chooses, the change may be unsuccessful.

Fig. 58 Tempi or sequence changes – involving flying changes from every four strides down to every stride, can be exhilarating for both horse and rider. This illustration shows the horse changing leads at every stride

Size of Strides

Each change stride should be of similar size to the canter, not much bigger and certainly no smaller as this would mean that the horse was either losing impulsion or not going forwards. A change bigger than the canter stride is acceptable as if it is a result of the energy from within the horse, this gives more expression to the movement.

The changes are a really exciting part of the training, but it is a mistake to get carried away and overdo work on them. Time is the essence and much patience will be needed. Riders should be prepared to take years rather than months on establishing good quality changes, with which the horse can cope mentally and physically. As the change of leg, the bend and the aids from the rider gradually co-ordinate the result will seem effortless and smooth and, like all training exercises when they come right, exhilarating.

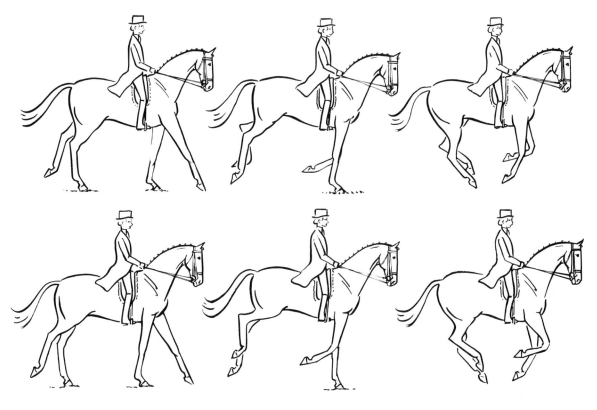

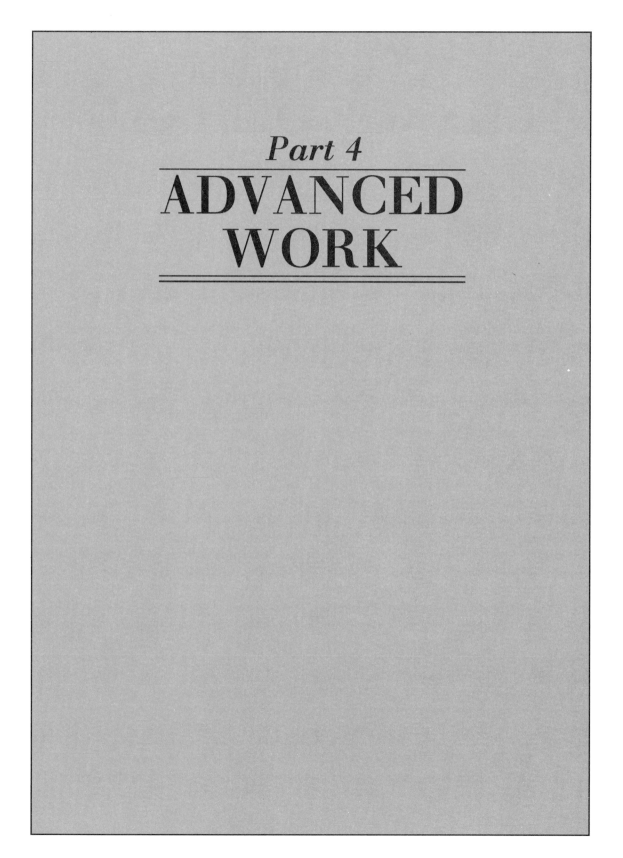

Part 4
ADVANCED WORK

18

COUNTER CHANGE OF HAND IN CANTER

Training a horse to Advanced Level normally runs over approximately a five-year period. The first two years are occupied in teaching, establishing and consolidating the basics, and beginning the work for the middle standard (Medium to lower Advanced tests). The next period is to confirm all lateral work and changes in the air, pirouettes, extensions and collection, and start work on piaffe and passage. The final stage is to be able to ride the Grand Prix work consistently well and to develop test riding technique at this level.

Entering into the final phase requires a high degree of collection, submission and accuracy. The collection at Advanced Level must have well established impulsion, which has to be contained by the rider for controlled use in various forms for the different exercises. For instance, a forward form of expressed energy is shown in extensions, whereas a highly collected form is needed for a canter pirouette. Great power from the hindquarters and collection combined give the horse the ability to passage and also to lower the haunches and sustain a number of steps in piaffe.

The collection and controlled impulsion is only possible if the horse has learned to submit to his rider's aids. He must do this willingly and without resistance. Any objections will be manifest by tension in

the poll, the lower jaw, the neck and the back and loins. Tension in the poll may enable the horse to evade the aids by refusing to flex laterally or vertically, making it impossible to initiate a bend or bring him onto the bit correctly. He may also tilt his head (Fig.59). Tension in the lower jaw may be directly affected by the poll tension but, in addition, the horse may evade the bit by gripping it with his molars, crossing the jaw, putting his tongue out or over the bit, leaning on his rider's hands or generally putting his head where he likes. He will soon find in this circumstance that he is in charge of the situation and not the rider. He can also use his neck adversely by putting it too high, too low, holding it rigidly, curving it in one direction while he veers away from it and so on. Tension in the back and loins prevent true engagement of the hindquarters being possible. Muscles held against the rider's seat make the horse a 'hard' ride and stop him swinging his back. Also it is impossible to get good lateral bends or flexions. All stiffness or resistances will affect the purity of the gaits and can cause unlevel steps, four time canters, loss of rhythm and irregularities. Thus the quality of the work may be spoilt.

Of course all these faults should have been met and eradicated in the early training so that by the time the horse

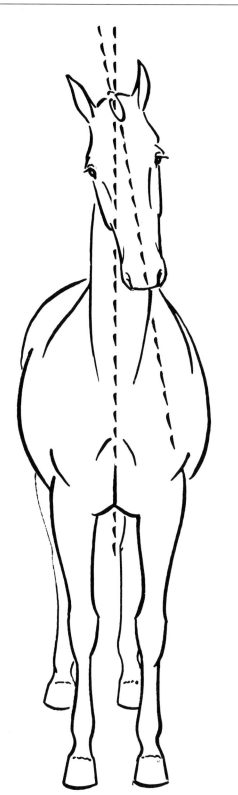

reaches Grand Prix they do not apply.

From correct obedience it will be possible to obtain the sort of accuracy necessary for advanced work. The horse will be finely tuned to the aids so that he will respond to almost imperceptible directions from his rider. As a result of the controlled impulsion and collection, he will be in a position to comply at once to any command and because of supreme suppleness and submission can perform with ease and grace, flowing smoothly from one movement to another. This fluency will be marked by clear cadence in all gaits, which do not falter through the transitions and which can show clearly the beginning and end of each movement.

Counter Change of Hand in Canter

Work on the counter changes of hand in trot and in canter will already have been going on for some time, first simply changing from one direction to another, i.e. half pass to the left followed by half pass to the right and vice versa. When this exercise becomes fluent, it will be necessary to teach what is commonly known as the zig-zag. This is a series of half passes to left and right, with appropriate alterations of bend. When performed in canter, it involves flying changes of leg as well.

To obtain a single counter change of hand is relatively easy if the horse thoroughly understands the half pass, although time to allow the change of bend should be carefully planned so that the bend remains true. It is also important to be sure that bends in both directions equal each other. When the horse is learning, he may find it difficult to change the bend over a short distance. If there is any problem, it may be useful to explain to him what you want in walk. This can also be done in the zig-zag.

Fig. 59 Tilting – the horse may try to evade the bend by tilting his head

Tests demand a variety of counter changes, from one change of direction to as many as five in canter in the Grand Prix, with a precise number of strides to each side of the centre line. Even where the steps are not specified, as in trot, a distance from the centre line is given, for example three metres to either side of the centre line. In training, the rider will learn to judge three metres and should count the number of steps it takes to reach the right place **(Fig.60)**. From then on, providing the impulsion and collection are consistent, the number of steps will be a good guide and will assist accuracy. If the horse is equally supple on both reins, the number of steps taken to one side of the centre line should be the same as to the other.

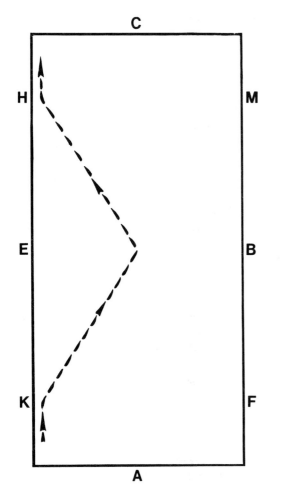

Judging distances

It can be very confusing for the more novice rider to work out exactly where he has to be in relation to the arena during the zig-zags. Although he must judge the distance from the centre line, he also needs to know how forward he should go and how sideways. Although it is desirable that an equal number of steps are taken, the accuracy of the movement is more important.

In canter, position is even more relevant as the number of strides is specified; for instance, from the centre line four strides to the right, eight to the left, eight to the right and four to the left **(Fig.61)**. These strides must be ridden accurately. If a counter change is ridden from the centre line to the side of the school returning to the centre, in this instance the number of strides is unspecified. Because the canter has to be retained, the horse must perform a change of leg in the air to be able to change direction. This change of leg would normally be done on the first stride of the new direction. For example, the fourth stride to the right is ridden straighter and more forward in order to be able to prepare the bend for the new direction to the left. The change then occurs on the next stride, as the horse starts the left half pass. If the horse is correctly suppled, he will be able to change his leg and the bend almost simultaneously, but because of his length the preparation is still necessary. At Grand Prix level, the exercise is very tight. It must be extremely fluent to fit into the arena, and the horse's ability to execute flying changes must be very well established.

Fig. 60 Counter change of hand in trot – 3m either side of the centre line. It is important to be aware of the invisible line!

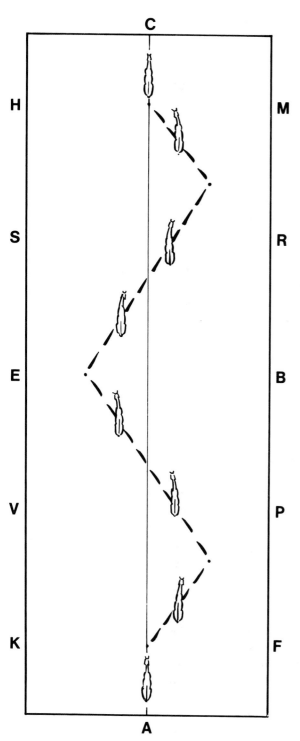

Positioning the horse

During all counter changes of hand, the positioning of the horse is important to the function of the exercise. The positioning is the placing of the horse's forehand, directing it to the point of arrival and not losing sight of this objective in the effort of trying to go sideways. If the forehand is properly placed and the horse will curve his hindquarters round the rider's inside leg for the bend, these factors, combined with different degrees of collection, make the exercise possible. It must be stressed that the use of the rider's inside leg is of utmost importance in gaining ground via impulsion, maintaining bend and in arriving at the designated point. The outside leg should not be thought of as merely pushing the horse sideways but, as already stated, it curves the hindquarters around the rider's inside leg to make more bend, helps general control and assists the inside leg to create impulsion.

So often in lateral work riders use the inside rein too much in an effort to obtain bend. This only prevents forward movement and freedom of the shoulder. A good exercise to test yourself is to begin the exercise and then 'give and retake' the inside rein to discover whether you can maintain it. As the exercise should have been used regularly during training for example on circles and corners, and in shoulder-in, it will not be a surprise to the horse but something he will accept readily.

The Grand Prix standard may demand a severe counter change of hand which will require a lot of collection and suppleness if it is to flow. Obedience is of the essence in this exercise as any resistance to the

Fig. 61 Counter change of hand in canter – four strides to right, eight to left and four to right

aids will not only cause ugliness but also bring both parties much vexation. Loss of impulsion and engagement in any exercise makes work laborious but in this one, particularly, it can be devastating.

In all lateral work the greatest asset is a correct gait, with good moments of suspension during which the horse gains ground. If the gaits are true, the difficulty of the different exercises will be lessened and providing the hind-quarters are at no time allowed to precede the forehand, the horse will be capable of executing his rider's wishes.

RIDER'S TIP

The rider must of course help the horse all he can with clear aids and good preparation. He can also help by keeping his weight slightly onto his inside seatbone for direction and making sure that the upper body does not lean away from the direction to which he is going.

The hand and leg aids must be continually controlling the position of the forehand and the bend. They cannot be a static entity although too much movement is unattractive and unnecessary.

19
SERPENTINES

There are a variety of serpentines, or loops, which can be performed in the school; some suitable for the novice horse and the more difficult to add to the training for Advanced Level.

In all trot serpentines, a change of bend is required. In canter, the bend should be maintained to the leading leg at all times. Serpentines vary in their requirements concerning changes of leg. For example, one loop may be to true lead and the next to counter lead, but there need be no dismay over variations providing the horse has been correctly prepared and is obedient.

Serpentines in Trot

Beginning with serpentines in trot, the most simple ones are as in **Fig.62**, where the horse has only to make shallow deviations from the centre line with minimal change of bend. Because of the comparative lack of difficulty, there is time for the bend to be altered gradually. The horse will have been prepared for such an exercise by having been ridden through loops of varying depths on the school long side, by half circles within circles or returning to the track at different markers all of which involve changes of flexion and bend **(Fig.63)**. In a short (40-metre) arena, a

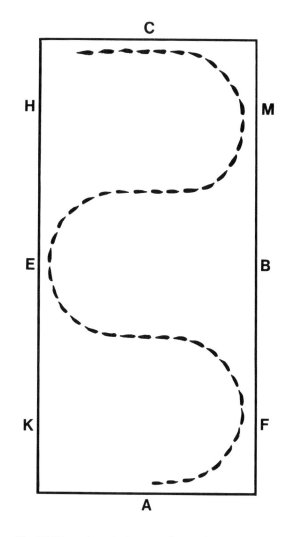

Fig. 62 Three-loop trot serpentine – short arena

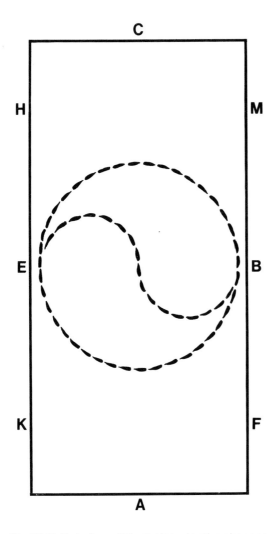

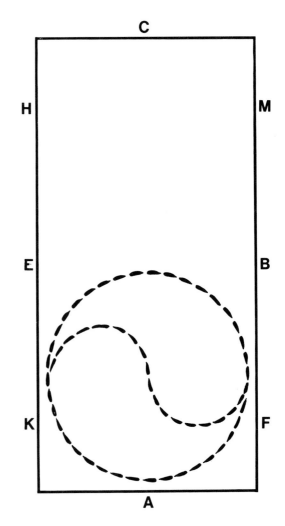

Fig. 63 Half circles within circles – involve changes of flexion and bend

serpentine will normally be of three loops, but five is possible in a long (60-metre) arena. It is very important to control the horse with precision as it is very easy for one shoulder or the other to take too much weight or for the hindquarters to swing. If the bend is true, the horse will be balanced and the hindfeet will follow the track of the forefeet. The shoulder-in aids will help the rider to position the horse correctly, help him with the balance and keep the horse 'upright', in other words prevent the horse leaning on the inside rein and/or leg. If the aids are reversed carefully for changes of direction, the exercise should be easier to ride and will flow. As in all exercises, the use of the rider's inside leg for keeping up impulsion is of paramount importance.

The more troubling serpentine is as in **Figs.64–65** where loss of impulsion, balance, rhythm and carriage often occurs. First concentrate on the gait, making certain that it remains correct. Then ride the movement accurately, being sure that you do not give away ground by allowing the horse to cut in. Using the shoulder-in aids for the positioning of each direction as you cross the centre line should once more assist the entire movement.

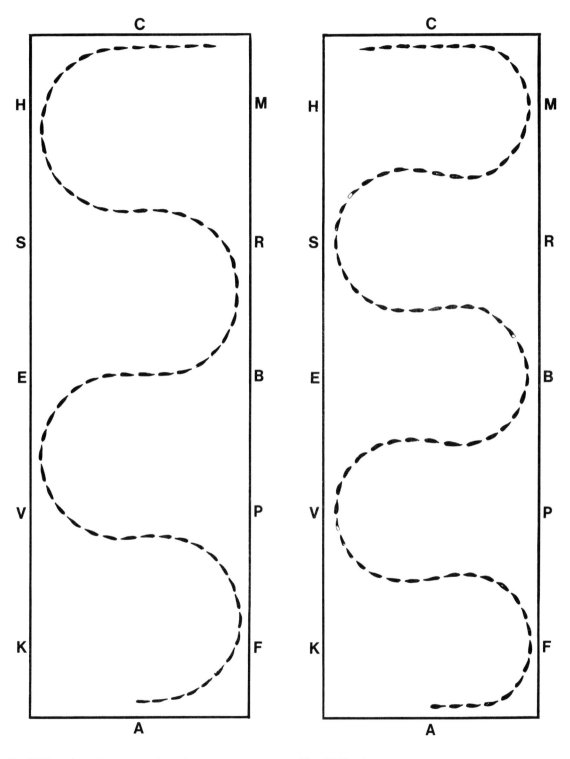

Fig. 64 Four-loop trot serpentine – long arena   *Fig. 65* Five-loop canter serpentine – long arena

Medium trot

These exercises are normally ridden in working trot but in some more advanced tests all or part of a serpentine may be ridden in medium trot. This requires a lot of skill from the rider and a good degree of engagement, balance and suppleness from the horse.

Serpentines in Canter

The serpentine in **Fig.65** is the one in canter with changes in the air on the centre line. In most tests this would involve a single change but many riders in free style tests like to do a sequence crossing the centre line (for instance changes at every stride) which looks most effective. For the purpose of this explanation, however, I only propose to discuss a single change.

The lead up to being able to perform the entire exercise would be to ride two loops with one change in the middle. The important part of the exercise is positioningg the horse so that it is easy for him to change leading legs. This means lining him up for a good approach. Therefore time must be allowed for the horse to come round the first curve then straighten (on shoulder-in aids to the leading leg). The rider asks for the change to take place directly over the centre line, continuing straight on shoulder-in aids to the new leading leg and then make the next curve. When this can be accomplished equally well in both directions, proceed to the next loop and so on. If control of the forehand is uppermost in the rider's mind and the horse is obedient to the leg aids, the exercise should be pleasant to ride and good to watch.

Counter canter

The more complicated serpentine depends upon the ability of the rider to keep his horse in a satisfactory counter canter. Once more, the purity of the gait comes first but is easily impaired by poor engagement or enforced collection. The horse must be capable of carrying himself in a high state of collection, without any restriction from the rider. This especially applies to the use of the inside rein, a factor so frequently guilty of restricting the horse's freedom.

Preparation

The positioning on shoulder-in aids is the main ingredient for success in this exercise. Start with two loops only. This will mean beginning in counter canter in order to change leg to counter canter. Because in this exercise the change of bend must occur in such a small space of time, it may be advisable to straighten the horse for a stride before the change.

RIDER'S TIP – SERPENTINE IN COUNTER CANTER

Simple loops, circles and half circles will have brought the horse to the stage of readiness. He should also have learned much about lowering his hindquarters, enabling him to take his balance by putting weight onto the haunches.

The forehand should be light, with no reliance on the rider's hands. The strides must be very collected, with a good moment of suspension.

The suspension allows the change of leg to take place, so it is crucial to the success of the exercise.

20

CANTER PIROUETTES

In learning to take weight onto the hind-quarters, being accomplished in collection and light in hand, the horse will be fully prepared for the development of canter pirouettes. This entails progressing from half-pirouettes to full pirouettes **(22a,22b)** and eventually to double pirouettes, which are used in freestyle (Kur) tests. The half-pirouettes, if established satisfactorily, will have taught the horse how to 'sit', engaging his hindquarters well under his body to lift his forehand. At all times during any pirouette, the correctness of the gait (three beats) is most important.

Preparation

Collection Plus

During training, the horse will have developed an ability to execute an extra-collected canter, enabling him to bounce almost on the spot. (This is necessary not only for pirouettes, but also as preparation for halts from canter.) This 'collection plus' is obtained from extra engagement of the hindquarters, impulsion and complete submission to the aids and is achieved by a succession of half halts. Be sure that you keep the canter a true three beats, straight (by positioning) and that at any moment you can go forwards.

Control over the horse needs to be exact but never restrictive. Aids should not suffocate the movement but allow freedom within precision. The inside leg, responsible for the trueness of the gait, impulsion and bend, will send the energy to the outside hand, which controls the speed and collection. This hand will be chiefly responsible, for the control of the energy while the inside hand is indicating direction and keeping flexion. Both legs control the size of the strides during the turns, making sure that the width of the strides are equal to each other. An inordinately larger stride, intermingled with smaller ones, may cause loss of balance and possibly resistance. Both hands will assist in bringing the forehand round and in maintaining an upright position of the horse's shoulders, i.e. preventing the horse falling onto one or the other.

Size of pirouette

The size of the pirouette may be hard to assess unless you are experienced, but although it should be at a designated marker, the horse must not be allowed to pivot behind but must remain fractionally forward and always on the aids **(Fig.66)**. In training for the full pirouette, it will be ridden rather large at first, with the hind feet describing a tiny circle.

22a A rider attempting a left canter pirouette but coming up against resistance – the horse has become hollow and above the bit

22b A canter pirouette to the right ridden correctly – the pirouette shows a calm horse with correct bend remaining round in outline. The inside hind leg (off hind) is in a good position for supporting the weight during the turn

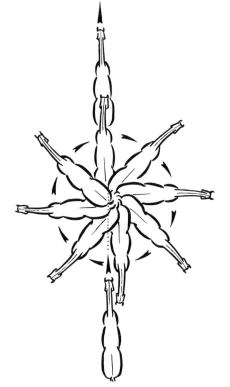

Fig. 66 Pirouette on the circle

Approaches and Departures

All approaches and departures should be clearly defined. For instance, an approach from a quarter marker to X must not deviate as the pirouette draws closer. Hold the horse straight and keep him to the line by the use of shoulder-in positioning. As the aids are applied for 'collection plus' just prior to the turn, the control of the forehand is most important if the turn is to be executed properly. Any swinging of the quarters at this point will throw him out of balance. The pirouette will not be complete unless the departure is on the correct line. Control is frequently mislaid at this point and the positioning of the shoulders forgotten, but if all is remembered, the horse will be able to conclude the exercise satisfactorily.

Pirouettes from a circle

Pirouettes can be taught to the horse in various places in the school, but quite an easy way to begin full pirouettes is from a circle, where he is already bent round the inside leg of the rider and can be collected readily. It is also reasonably easy to come out of the turn at any moment if necessary, and continue the circle which gives the rider the opportunity to make any corrections to balance, bend, collection before trying again.

Much of the success of a pirouette depends on good maintenance of the bend and the engagement of the inside hind leg of the horse coming well under the body to take the weight. Lack of suppleness will cause many problems for both parties.

RIDER'S TIP – BE PREPARED

Once the horse understands the exercise, or as soon as he feels the preparation aids, he may anticipate and try to start the turn. Be prepared, so that you can avert the possibility before it starts.

PROBLEMS WITH CANTER PIROUETTE

Fault	*Solutions*
• Canter loses correct sequence • Losing impulsion • Horse resists hands – above or behind bit • Resisting leg – kicking at or changing behind • Losing bend • Hindquarters swinging out • Changing tempo • Uneven strides • Humping back against rider's seat • Not lowering quarters • Lifting forehand – rearing round • Pirouette too large • Pirouette too small – stepping back	Many faults occur because the correct sequence of steps is lost. This is generally due to loss of impulsion. Make sure you prepare adequately. • Hollowing and resistance may be due to the rider restricting the gait so the improvement can be made by making the horse go forwards in a rounder outline. • Resistances to aids are best dealt with by riding onto a circle until the horse submits to the correct outline, impulsion and collection before attempting again. • Some problems happen because the approach or departure is not straight. A shoulder-in position before and after the pirouette should counteract this. • Lack of balance during the pirouette causes resistances. It is up to the rider to 'prepare' adequately.

21
PIAFFE AND PASSAGE

Piaffe

Piaffe is a collected, elevated and cadenced trot on the spot. The quarters are lowered, hocks active and well engaged, giving freedom, lightness and mobility to the shoulders and forehand. Each diagonal pair of feet is raised and returned to the ground alternately with a slightly prolonged suspension.

Earlier in the training, piaffe steps should have been introduced in order to start to prepare the horse for later work and to teach the horse greater engagement of the hindquarters. During this work, the horse will have learned to accept a high degree of collection and be free from resistance in order to produce the required steps. He will not have been asked to piaffe on the spot, but will have remained slightly forward. He will have been brought to the piaffe steps by a series of half halts and in all probability he will have started this from a collected walk. He must remain straight and rounded in outline, taking even steps. The hindquarters should lower slightly, enabling the forehand to be raised, thereby lightening the load on the horse's shoulders.

The hind feet should spring from one to the other, well under the horse's body, lifting a little higher than the coronet, while the foreleg should lift so that the hoof reaches the centre of the cannon bone on the opposite foreleg **(23)**. The raised leg, from knee to fetlock, should be vertical to the ground. Each diagonal pair of legs should be raised and lowered to the ground alternately, showing a discernible cadence and moment of suspension.

Aids for piaffe

The aids for the piaffe can vary, as some riders use an alternate leg action and others a 'tapping' action with both legs at the same time. Both are satisfactory, providing they do not allow the hindquarters to swing.

Developing piaffe

Once the horse understands what is required of him, the piaffe can be developed. A greater number of steps may be asked for, gradually decreasing their length. Any resistance to hand or leg should be corrected instantly, as if the horse learns to evade the aids, he will put himself in a position of control and will be able to avoid the exercise.

23 *(Overleaf)* Although this horse is being asked for piaffe the hind-quarters are not being lowered enough. The off hind should be level with the coronet of the near hind while the near fore should be nearer to the centre of the cannon bore of the off fore

PIAFFE IN HAND

To develop the piaffe further, you may take the horse 'in hand' – that is teach him from the ground using a lunge rein on a cavesson over the bridle with side reins attached to the saddle, and a long whip to tap him on the hind legs just above the hock or sometimes on the buttocks. This action of the whip will send the impulsion forward to be controlled by the trainer holding the lunge rein on the cavesson so that he can regulate the size and height of the steps.

Others will prefer to train the horse ridden, perhaps helped by an assistant with a schooling whip. Both methods are useful, but the aim is for the horse to understand and respond to the rider's aids. Many riders are at a loss in the arena without the help of their assistants!

PROBLEMS WITH PIAFFE

Fault
Some horses will try to perform piaffe with the weight still on their shoulders, bringing the croup up instead of lowering it.

Solution
Reconsider your position and check that your half halts and transitions are correct.

Passage

Passage is a very collected, very elevated and cadenced trot (**Fig.67**). There is a pronounced engagement of the quarters, accentuated flexion of knees and hocks and graceful elasticity of movement. Each diagonal pair of feet are raised and returned to the ground with even cadence and a prolonged suspension.

The passage should be a natural development, resulting from a high degree of controlled impulsion, which, if contained, gives the steps more height. It is arrived at by collecting the gait and using half halts in the same manner as for piaffe, but with different aids and more energy. To differentiate from piaffe, in passage the rider may use a firmer leg in the rhythm of the steps. Ask for only a few steps to start with and then resume the trot, being very

Fig. 67 **Passage** – Here the moment of suspension is pronounced. The steps must retain a regular rhythm, demanding sustained balance from the horse and rider

24 In passage

careful to keep an exact rhythm. As time goes by, the horse may be asked to perform more steps in passage, until he can maintain the exercise for the movements required **(24)**.

The toe of the raised foreleg should be level with the middle of the cannon bone of the opposite foreleg. The toe of the raised hind leg should be slightly above the fetlock joint of the other hind leg. Each diagonal pair of legs should come to the ground alternately, with a prolonged moment of suspension.

Transitions from Piaffe to Passage

When the horse can 'hold' the passage well, you will want to put together piaffe and passage. Often there can be difficulty while the horse is learning, but providing the aids are clear, and the horse is brought carefully and gradually from one to the other, the problems should not become troublesome. If the horse becomes agitated, starts to swing from side to side, does not go forwards when asked or at worst runs back, remain calm and go back a stage until the horse becomes more receptive.

To bring this work to a state of near perfection can take considerable time, perhaps years rather than months, but much depends on the knowledge of the rider and the horse's natural ability.

RIDER'S TIP – BE CONSISTENT

One danger is that having learned the passage, the horse may use it as an evasion to going forwards properly. You must be strict with yourself as well as the horse in making the difference between trot and passage very clear and not allowing any hesitation to occur.

Always be consistent, and be confident of the rhythm for both trot and passage.

22
DRESSAGE TO MUSIC

Dressage to music has become very popular both with competitors and the public who find it good entertainment, bringing a different slant to something aesthetically serious. Making a programme and fitting it to music is a simple idea, but the actual execution is a different matter. The music is the most troublesome part of the operation. Tunes that will match the gaits of one particular horse are hard to find and their discovery may take many hours of listening to tapes and records. Anything considered suitable should be taken into the arena where you can check whether they complement your horse's paces. Impulsion must not be sacrificed, and if the match is not obvious, the performance will not succeed.

Freestyle Programme (kur)

Some riders choose music with no obvious beat and some simply ride to music with no apparent relevance. This is not the object. The whole point of dressage to music is the interpretation. The dressage rider should consider her programme in the same way as ice skaters, who include variations in mood and feel and put in a difficult exercise at a crescendo or during a change of tempo. The object will be to present a technically correct performance with a stimulating, exciting musical accompaniment.

The choice of programme will depend on the standard of training. It will be a freestyle programme (Kur) so that the stipulated movements may be fitted together in any order as the rider wishes. There will be certain compulsory movements at each standard which must be included, but otherwise the rider has carte blanche and may concentrate on displaying his horse's good points and avoid those at which he is not especially talented. The test must be proficient yet have flair, so a certain amount of risk in tackling more challenging movements is desirable. Of course, it would be unwise to follow this policy unless the horse is competent and his work well established.

Programmes on the whole look better from a judging point of view if they are symmetrical. They are also easier to balance when working them out. A lopsided test is extremely unattractive as are too many movements which are done going away from the judge. Clearly, there must be some to ensure good use of the arena, but the movements which need the emphasis, such as half passes and shoulder-in, should, if possible, be ridden towards C.

As the timing for freestyle tests is quite tight, do not waste time on movements which will not help to gain marks. Take the compulsory movements, then choose the most difficult movements for that standard, and try to put them into a pattern. Plan your tests on paper first and then ride it to see if it fits into the time. The timing begins at X at the first salute and ends at the final one. A warning is sometimes given a minute before the time runs out and then a final signal is given at which point even if he has not finished his programme the rider must turn onto the centre line and salute. Anyone much under the time allowed may be penalized.

Alterations may have to be made at home several times to get the programme to fit the time. In the switch from one tape to another without a pause or hiccup, modern equipment is invaluable; a machine with two tapes, one of which can be faded as the other is brought in, and so on. The tape completed, not only should you learn your programme inside out and back to front but also it is helpful to sit and listen to the tape over and over again remembering exactly what you do at which point so that during the performance you can be precise.

RIDER'S TIP – SURFACES

Different surfaces can present a problem in that some are more holding than others and this can play havoc with your careful preparation. However, if you are clever you will be able to make some adjustments to the collection and impulsion which should keep you on course.

In the event of a real miscalculation be ready to ad lib with a smile on your face as if that was exactly what you meant to do!

RIDER'S TIP – MUSIC

If you have a friend with a good knowledge of music, why not enlist his or her help? Alternatively, a member of your local music club or orchestra may have an interest in dressage and be pleased to advise and research suitable material for your programme. Be aware of copyright restrictions.

Part 5
COMPETITIVE DRESSAGE

23
PREPARATION FOR YOUR FIRST COMPETITION

Quite soon following the preliminary stages of training, you may wish to take your horse to his first show, but although you may feel that his work is coming along well, it is wise to check his preparation thoroughly. There are several essential aspects of the horse's education which should not be ignored.

Ride in Company

If your horse is kept at a large livery yard or equestrian centre, he may be quite used to working in company. If not, he may have to learn that despite the excitement of being with other horses, he is still required to concentrate and be obedient to his rider. You will need to arrange several 'get togethers' with other riders to teach your young horse how to behave, to control his own exuberance and to ignore the bad behaviour of other horses. Riding club rallies and lessons provide excellent opportunities for introducing your horse to a wide variety of situations and circumstances, as well as valuable instruction.

Ride on Different Surfaces

If you are one of the lucky ones you may have an all-weather surface or indoor manège to school on at home, but at shows, particularly at lower levels, the competition arena may leave much to be desired! Prepare your horse for any eventuality. Grass arenas can be rock hard and slippery, muddy and slippery, or simply deep mud. Your horse's regularity, rhythm and balance will be adversely affected by such conditions, but if he has been accustomed at home to any type of going, he will be able to get through the test.

Weather

Not only should you be prepared for the underfoot conditions, but also rain driving sideways in torrents, gales, snowstorms and raging heat. Whenever the weather seems intolerable for training, part of your discipline will be to make yourself work in it so that you are never caught out.

Hazards

Horseboxes, the judge's car, white arena boards, flags, music, tents, caravan awnings, birds, other animals are just a few of the hazards with which your horse has to contend. The more he has seen before he is asked to compete, the less likely he is to be upset by hazards. If his eyes are popping out on stalks because he is bewildered by a host of new sights and sounds, he is unlikely to be concentrating on his rider.

Loading and Travelling

Ensure that your horse will go into and out of a horsebox or trailer calmly and willingly. It will not help you to ride a good test if either you or your horse has been stressed by an unpleasant journey. Take your horse on a few short journeys so that he becomes used to travelling, and for your first competition, do not travel too far. Remember to drive slowly and carefully, especially round bends, as your horse has no way of anticipating and preparing himself for a change of direction. Allow plenty of time for stopping, and pulling away from a junction.

Know the Rules and the Test

Check the rules for your class, including any restrictions on rider's dress and horse's tack.

Learn the test thoroughly. This can be done in several ways. Some people learn the test as they would a poem. Others draw an arena onto a piece of paper and then go over the movements with a pen until the test is committed to memory. You could walk the test on foot. Riding the test should be limited to a few trials, as horses quickly learn to anticipate the movements: this can work to your advantage if you happen to have forgotten what comes next, but can be disastrous if the horse remembers a test slightly different from the one you are riding!

If you have great difficulty remembering, or are riding in several tests, you could ask a helper to call the test for you. Practise this at home if possible, as an inexperienced caller could be more of a distraction than a help.

Study the test

It is not enough just to know the test. It is vital to know exactly what marks are given by the judge so that you can partly assess for yourself how you are progressing. For example, there may be 10 marks for a medium trot between M and F which include the transitions. Or the 10 marks may be for the medium trot, the transitions, collected trot between F and A and a transition to walk. Many misunderstandings of the judging occur because the competitor has not taken these factors into account.

LOADING SAFELY

Prepare the transport
- Park in a sensible, safe place where the ramp is not too steep.
- Swing or remove the partition for young, nervous or difficult horses.

Prepare the horse
- Put on travelling boots and bandages.
- Use common sense with regard to temperature and weather. Do not overheat the horse by putting on too warm a rug.
- Be patient. Allow the horse time to look into the transport and go in slowly.
- Be prepared to be firm if necessary.
- Do not tie the horse up until the ramp is up (and do not lower the ramp until the horse is untied).

24
YOUR HORSE'S FIRST SHOW

Turnout

Having gone to a good deal of trouble to prepare your horse, you must then also present him properly for the show by turning him out as well as you can. Imagine you are entering a show hack class, and, apart from saddlery, turn him out accordingly **(25)**.

Rider's turnout

Of course, it is equally important for the rider to be well turned out. Clothes should fit well and comply with the rules of the National Federation for your particular class **(25)**. Do check whether spurs and whips are allowed. There may also be a stipulation regarding colour of boots,

25 *(Right)* A horse and rider correctly turned out for Advanced Dressage competitions. Note the pulled and trimmed mane plaited along the off-side of the crest. Plaiting bands give a neat result, but plaits may be sown in. Hairspray will keep them in place

26 *(Left)* Informal dress

breeches and gloves. Clean clothes and shiny boots, gloves and a hairnet (if female) are essential. Any makeup should be discreet. Remember that in an overall picture of horse and rider, it can be a mistake to draw the judge's eye to any one particular aspect.

Saddlery

Correct saddlery for a specific class will be laid down in the rule book, but whatever tack you are using, it should fit the horse, fit you, be in good condition and be clean **(Fig.68)**. Many people use a square white saddlecloth. No bandages, boots or martingales will be allowed in the competition, so if you use them for riding in, remember to take them off in plenty of time before the test.

Fig. 68 Saddle – Make sure it fits you and your horse. A dressage saddle has a straighter cut than a general purpose or jumping saddle

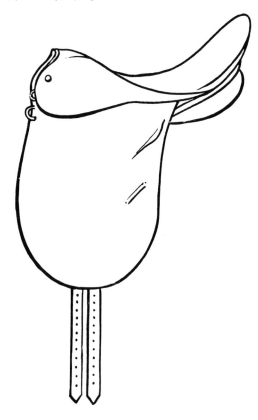

Checklists

Many riders have recurring nightmares about leaving behind at home a vital item of tack or clothing! Clearly, before the show, all will have been prepared and cleaned, ensuring every item fits and is comfortable. Having once been caught out with only a dressing gown to drive home in, everything else being sopping wet, I would now recommend a complete change of clothes, together with towels. Similarly, be prepared for the opposite weather from that you set off in. I have several times suffered agonies in boiling sun when all I have taken to the show to change into were fur boots and a roll neck sweater. Keep a comprehensive list to help you remember absolutely everything! **(Figs.69–71)**

At the Show

Aim to arrive in plenty of time, to allow you to ride in, study the arena and collect your number **(27)**. When you arrive, ensure your horse is well. If you are on your own, it may be advisable to report to the show secretary, collect your number and confirm your starting time before you unload your horse.

Study the arena

Arenas are rarely as flat as they look! If at all possible, before your class, study the surface to see where the ground is uneven. There are frequently holes at X which can bury a potentially good halt or hideously interrupt a lengthened trot on a diagonal. Any slight variation in the ground should be noticed and accounted for by careful riding. Sand surfaces can be very deep and

27 This horse has been clearly numbered for the judges' reference. Note the fitting of the bridle (browband slightly large) and how even the plaits are

Fig. 69 **Snaffle bits** – only certain types of bits are allowed in dressage competitions: check the rules to make sure you comply.

f Eggbutt snaffle with or without cheeks

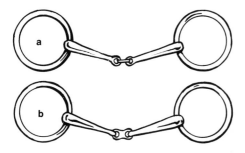

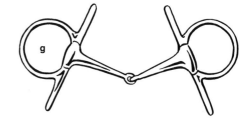

g

a and **b** Snaffles with double-jointed mouthpiece

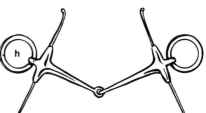

c Snaffle with jointed mouthpiece

h Snaffle with cheeks

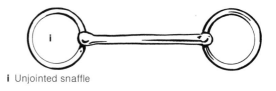

d Racing snaffle

i Unjointed snaffle

e Snaffle with upper cheeks

j Rubber snaffle

holding if extremely wet. They can also hold the water causing pools on the surface; distracting to say the least as you flounder through them. Some arenas based on woodchips are lovely when dry but can be very slippery if too wet. Unless you are first to ride, you may have the opportunity to watch one or two tests to see how the arena rides.

Another point to consider is the position of the arena. For example, your horse may move more freely in the direction of the horseboxes, but need riding more strongly in the other direction.

RIDER'S TIP – NUMBERS

If numbers are to be worn round the waist, take a length of tape that matches the colour of your jacket, to replace the white tape of the number creating an ugly white line.

Sometimes the number can be cut down so that it is smaller and neater. Check that it is worn straight, and is not hanging to one side.

Fig. 70 Curb & Bridoon bits

Curb bits

Bridoon bits

a Ordinary bridoon

b Bridoon with two joints

c Eggbutt bridoon

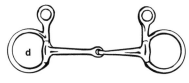

d Bridoon with cheeks

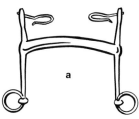

a Half moon curb

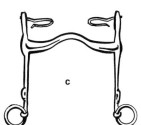

c Curb with curved cheeks and port

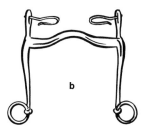

b Curb with loops for lipstrap on the cheeks and with port

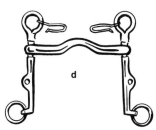

d Curb with port and sliding mouthpiece

f Cover for curb chain – may be rubber or leather

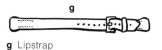

g Lipstrap

e Curb chain

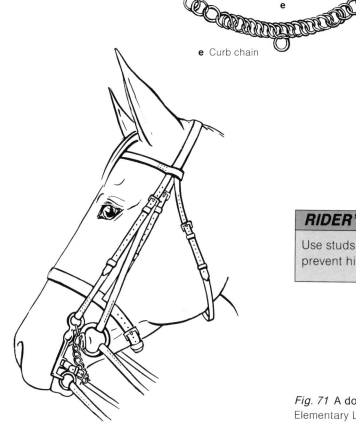

RIDER'S TIP

Use studs in your horse's shoes to help prevent him from slipping.

Fig. 71 **A double bridle** – may be used at and above Elementary Level – it is compulsory at Advanced Level

SHOW CHECK LISTS

Horse

- Bridle
  - snaffle or double stated in test
  - correct noseband
  - spare rein
- Saddle
  - stirrups
  - leathers
  - spare leather
  - girth
  - spare girth
  - numnah or saddle cloth
- Schooling whip
- Spurs
- Spare headcollar and rope
- Lunge cavesson
- Lunge rein
- Lunge whip
- Boots
- Spare leg bandages
- Spare tail bandages
- First aid equipment
- Set of shoes for travelling abroad
- Horse passport/necessary papers
- Vaccination certificate
- Rugs, blankets, sheets etc, according to time of year
- Roller, surcingle
- Sponge
- Grooming kit
- Hoof oil
- Plaiting equipment
- Bucket
- Water
- Feed
- Haynet

Rider

- Top hat or cap
- Tail coat and/or jacket
- Hair net
- Stock or tie
- Pin
- Shirt
- Spare shirt (in case of wet or hot weather)
- Spare stock
- Gloves
- Breeches
- Spare breeches
- Pop socks for inside top boots
- Boots
- Boot pull
- Polish
- Raincoat
- Change of clothes
- Towel
- Money
- Flask
- Food
- Schedule and Passes
- Number if previously sent
- Directions to venue

Riding in

Riding in at your horse's first show will be a matter of trial and error, as you will have no idea of how your horse will react to the atmosphere. It is better to allow too much time than too little and run the risk of 'going over the top'.

Some riders like to lunge their horses for a while before mounting, but make sure your horse is totally obedient on the lunge before you attempt this in a large, open field with strange horses around.

Riding in before a competition should be like a ballet dancer's exercises before a performance: the aim is to have the horse attentive, willing to please, supple and warm, ready for the concentrated effort that will be asked of him. Choose a place away from too many other horses and riders and not in the direct view of the judges (they will be watching you while waiting for their next competitor). Work on large, simple circles and figures in walk and trot, with frequent changes of direction, until your horse is settled and listening to you, before beginning canter work.

When you have finished, remove any boots or bandages from your horse, make sure your dress is correct, and give a final polish to boots and tack, before riding towards the arena for your test. Aim to present yourself a minute or two before your given time. There may be a steward to call you forward. Ensure that the judge and his writer can see your number clearly, and do not start before the given signal.

Test Technique

Test technique really evolves from experience in riding many tests. Begin with a confident entry, smart salute and smile at the judge. Do not hurry, but take your time gathering your reins and moving off purposefully. Ride all movements and figures as accurately as possible. Points are lost for starting movements early or late at markers: the rider's shoulder should be level with the marker at the moment of transition. Make all transitions smooth, clear and precise.

A clever rider learns how to pick up marks by thoughtful riding. This can involve good preparation for movements, which sometimes can be started a little early to give the horse more time. It can also mean 'covering up' a horse's deficiency by not asking too much of him in a particular movement. A clever rider will never give away to the judge that his horse has a stiffness to one side by showing more bend on one rein than the other. On a small circle, if there are likely to be irregular steps for some reason, impulsion is dropped, so that the movement is easier for the horse. If a horse has a poor extended trot, the transitions are exaggerated to make the difference look greater. If a horse is taking too strong a hold, he is checked by the rider's hand on the side the judge cannot see.

This kind of cheating, for this is what it really is, should not be considered good dressage but nevertheless the more experienced rider will know the various ways to gain a better score. A more correct way is to train the horse properly so that cheating is not necessary, but a quick recovery sometimes is, and part of the technique is to be able to act quickly. For instance, a slip on uneven going or a shy can disturb the flow. The more trained the horse, the more quickly he will return to obedience, and the more experienced the rider, the less he or she will be flustered by a mistake and be able to proceed to the following movement.

Staying cool in such circumstances may be in the rider's character, in which case he is very fortunate but it can also be acquired by practice. Even trained horses have their tense days and this can be very distracting to the rider who is endeavouring to prevent the judge seeing this tenseness while physically coping with the complication. The rider's confidence in his ability to control his horse in various situations comes from the knowledge that his training has been correct and a total familiarity of the test he has to do. This should be so engraved in your mind that you should not have to worry about where to go in the arena, but be able to concentrate on the way your horse is going.

25

THE COMPETITOR'S POINT OF VIEW

Being competition-minded and desiring to win prizes is immensely compelling for some. I believe that people are either born to be competitive or not and that ambition is not something manufactured but is almost a need that has to be expressed. Those who wish to compete in dressage have their own particular drive which motivates them. They have been captured by an image to which they reach out. The discovery of training a horse excites their imagination, giving an aim which sometimes seems totally worthwhile and at others unbearably frustrating.

To be a successful competitor requires total commitment. The discipline to work every day is necessary, for both horse and rider learn by repetition. As a ballet dancer exercises at the bar every day or an athlete works out in a gymnasium or on the track, so must horse and rider develop together mentally and physically in a school. Such discipline helps to cope with the stress which all competitors face during test conditions.

Make sure that your training and fitness are up to scratch but also that you bring your horse to the right peak at the right time. Carefully plan your training programme, never losing sight of your ultimate and intermediate goals.

The role of a competitor is a position of great vulnerability both from the point of view of the training being tested and the fact that you are at the mercy of anything up to five judges spread around the arena!

This seemingly terrifying situation improves with practice but nevertheless it is almost impossible to hide anything from so many. With one judge it may be possible to cheat a little, stealing a bit of ground by enlarging a circle or giving the horse discreet verbal encouragement at the lower end of the arena. With five judges there is little opportunity for this sort of artfulness. The mental and physical tension is very wearing and even during a test it can suddenly seem all too much. Some riders will find that tension affects them before a test starts but then their adrenalin carries them through. Others will be calm beforehand but panic-struck the minute the bell goes!

These kind of problems do improve with experience, but even so there are few good riders who do not have some 'stage fright' before a big competition, and they would probably be no good if they did not. It is necessary to be keyed up to do well but not if it makes the brain and limbs seize up.

Psychological factors play an important part in a competition. One aspect that is most daunting is to look at other competitors and think that their horses are going ten times better than yours! Even if all the riders appear to ride brilliantly and their horses look wonderful, imagine that you and your horse probably look the same to them! Even if your arch rival goes in before you and is applauded out of the arena, try to be proud of your horse and give all your concentration to him. The judges may look grim – smile anyway! During the test do not catch their eye by mistake and do not be distracted by anything going on outside the arena, even if it is a loose horse galloping into the distance, a flock of sheep fast approaching or a helicopter hovering overhead! You should be absorbed by the horse and the test in a state of complete concentration.

Sometimes you will be aware beforehand that there are certain political goings on afoot. You may be aware that the powers that be are hoping you will go well enough to get into a team but the result must count or it may be someone else's horse that they want. You may have had a disagreement with one of the judges in the past and, to your great dismay, find him or her sitting at C. Do not be put off. Go in there and do your best and blow the politics! If you make a mistake, cover it up as quickly as possible and get on with the next movement.

Judges may seem aloof or unapproachable, but they are generally keen to help if asked. They are not intentionally biased and even if you think they do not like you or your horse, they are normally only trying to do their job, and a tough one it is too.

Sometimes you have to put up with a bad result. Try to take it on the chin, grit your teeth and go again. There will be occasions when your riding lets you down or the training was not so established as you thought. This is not a disaster, it happens to everyone and is all part of the game. The competition is a test, perfection an unattainable ideal for which we strive. Horses have their good and bad days and so do we. If we coincide on a good day that makes life wonderful.

RIDER'S TIP – OVERCOMING TENSION

- Confidence will come from knowing that you have prepared as well as possible for the event. This means (a) having established the standard of training necessary for each competition, and (b) knowing the test inside out.
- Allow enough time while riding in for your muscles to relax and mould themselves to the horse.
- Give all your concentration to the horse – this will enable you to ignore distractions.
- Remember to breathe! Tension often causes riders to hold their breath.
- Everyone is nervous before some or all competitions. Stage fright is almost essential to a good performance as it stimulates adrenalin. It is comforting to know that however cool others may look, they are probably feeling like you!
- Mistakes will happen – they do not make a disaster! Accepting the fact will help overcome them when they do occur. There is no need to be embarrassed – judges do understand.

26

THE DRESSAGE JUDGE'S POINT OF VIEW

Judges can be much misunderstood! This generally stems from the fact that from their position at the C marker, and indeed, from other positions, they can see details of which the rider may be unaware. As a result, the marks given are not always what the rider expects and quite often judges are blamed for giving poor marks, which when viewed from their vantage points, may well be justified. As riders, we think we know from the feel we are getting whether we have done the right thing but feel is not infallible and trained observation is worthy of serious consideration. Marks given by judges who believe what they have seen are not handed out lightly. Judging is a highly responsible and serious matter and most judges will have had many years of training learning to observe.

The Judge's Training

Correct training by other more experienced judges will help the aspiring judge to learn what is of more or lesser importance. She will discover where to place the emphasis, learn how to see correct gaits, assess collection and extension, value lateral work, determine the effectiveness of riders, learn to make helpful remarks, match comments to marks, give marks in the right place for the movements involved, follow the course of the test so that she knows instantly if the rider goes wrong, know all the rules, be impartial, mark what she sees on that day, be sympathetic but firm in her knowledge, have studied the physiological abilities of the horse, understand his mental capabilities and at all times try to be fair and consistent.

What is the judge looking for?

The question of where the judge puts the emphasis is sometimes confusing to the competitor who may have felt that his horse performed a sequence of movements very nicely but when he reads his mark sheets finds that the judges did not appear to agree. The answer to the riddle is in the difficulty of the main part of the sequence which is the part which will probably be the most important and therefore will take the judge's attention. This is not to say that the other movements are ignored, but the test will have been written to examine certain skills and these skills should be sufficiently established so that concentration can be given to the harder part of the exercise. It would be foolish for a rider to enter a competition where he himself cannot concentrate on the most difficult parts of it.

Discrepancies in the gaits

Much of the judges' training will have been to notice any discrepancies in the gaits. Her eye will be schooled to see unevenness, unlevelness, unsoundness or any irregularities of stride or rhythm. Unevenness can occur due to poor going or because the impulsion is variable and is usually momentary. Unlevelness is a distinctly different size step either in front or behind which may last for several strides or occur all the time on one rein. It may be due to the horse not going forwards, not accepting the aids properly or be because he is very one-sided. It may even have a more sinister cause, that of some kind of intermittent lameness in the feet, limbs or back. Sometimes a horse may be 'bridle lame': this is not a lameness as such but a resistance in the mouth, which has the effect of causing unlevelness.

The judge will have to discern whether the horse is lame or whether the cause is a training problem. This is sometimes very difficult to decide, but her responsibility is clear in that if the horse is irregular in his stride at any gait he will be penalised. Although sometimes the severity of the penalty is upsetting for a rider he should appreciate that the basis of training is founded upon pure, natural gaits and that their quality is of utmost importance.

The judge must also assess collection and extension. She will not reward a horse which is 'pulled together', instead of being properly collected, nor give high marks for exaggerated extensions which are unbalanced, wide behind or heavy in hand, nor be generous to those who do not show real differences between working, medium and extended paces.

In lateral work not only does the judge have to watch the feet of the horse but he must also note the bend, collection, impulsion, submission plus the quality of the gait, as well as transitions and accuracy.

Marks and Comments

With each movement, the judge may try to make a comment which will not only justify her mark but one which may give guidance to the rider. Because there is very little space and exceedingly little time, this comment is of necessity brief but it should correspond with the wording of marks available, i.e.

10	Excellent
9	Very good
8	Good
7	Fairly good
6	Satisfactory
5	Sufficient
4	Insufficient
3	Fairly bad
2	Bad
1	Very bad
0	Not executed

The judge has to be certain that she has given the mark at the right time (end of movement or series of movements). She must not be early or late as this will give a false result for that movement. She must notice whether a horse comes into the arena before the signal to start, whether it is wearing any forbidden saddlery, whether the rider is correctly attired and if whip or spurs are permissible. She must be thoroughly conversant with the test and be quick to correct if there is a mistake. If she is a senior judge, she may have to guide other judges, particularly if there is a query regarding some incident during the test.

A judge does not miss much! Sitting where she does, especially at C, every detail is painfully obvious. Those seemingly small wobbles on the centre line stand out like a sore thumb! A crooked halt, lack of bends in corners and circles, quarters in on the long side, late at markers, unsteadiness of rhythm or out-

line, use of the voice, poor aids, a bad position and many more points will be noted and must be assessed and marked. However, the judge only wants to see good riding and training so that she can give good marks. There is no satisfaction in marking people down. If everyone went well, it would make the judge's job a delight. It is making the choice between one poor mark and another which is such hard work.

Riders often complain about their marks and the judges, but although low marks are desperately disappointing, they must have happened for a reason, Judges do not dish them out for fun or because they do not like someone. Personalities do come into it, I grant, and sometimes a well-known rider may get a few more marks than he deserves but on the whole judges do try to mark what they see on the day. It is a poor judge who has to rely on someone else's view of a horse she judged last week!

Judges who have ridden to the standard they are judging are generally more satisfactory to competitors than those who have not. They will have the understanding and the feel of what is required and I do believe that this is highly advantageous. Those judges who have not or cannot ride the movements are more open to criticism and will find it harder to make their assessments. Their training should aim to include riding if possible, together with watching tests, continental trainers, top class riders, videos and any other visual aids available. They should attend conferences, read books and study the subject in depth if they are to be of value.

Agreement between judges does not always happen, sometimes there are fairly large differences. This is muddling to competitors, but by training and keeping

28 Judging – note the position of the judges at point B on the arena. In international competitions the others sit at M, C, H and E. The rider here is Jackie Farlow on Arnhem

up to date this can be avoided to a large extent. Judges should be willing to confer with each other on such occasions, to look at each other's point of view. If no common ground can be found, they may have to agree to differ as it must be accepted that the old saying of 'beauty is in the eye of the beholder' is inevitable at times. On the whole judges are doing their best and they are giving up their time for the good of the sport and without them competitors would be unable to compete!

RIDER'S TIP – WRITE FOR A JUDGE!

If your local riding club organises dressage shows, offer to write for a judge. The experience is usually interesting and enlightening.

27
INTERPRETING DRESSAGE MARK SHEETS

All dressage competitions are judged on mark sheets which are given to competitors at the end of the class **(Table 1)**. They contain not only the score but also comments relating to the points, good or bad, which affected the tests. These remarks may often seem merely critical but the reason for this is that the judge is only obliged to qualify lower marks with an explanation. The lower marks indicate a fault and this fault has to be described as briefly as possible partly because there is little space and partly because the judge and his writer are under pressure of time. This brevity often causes the comment to sound critical rather than constructive but the intention is to be helpful. Riders must realise also that a judge is there to assess and not to teach, although his remarks may give guidance. The meaning of some of the remarks may not be immediately clear and for this reason I set out some of the more usual ones.

Above the bit This is when the horse's head is above a horizontal line which if drawn would go along his back and through the withers towards the nose. In this position he is unbalanced, the bit is incorrectly placed in the mouth and there is little or no proper control. In fact it is a disaster, so if you get this remark, start again!

Against the hand This means that the horse is really in opposition to his rider and that, instead of yielding to the bit, he is resisting or leaning on it preventing any impulsion from taking him forwards. It is rather like riding at a closed door instead of an open one which you can go through.

Behind the bit This is an evasion to the bit when the horse hangs his head in an overbent position and does not go properly forwards when he would have to take the pressure.

Behind the leg Rather an ambiguous comment, but it means that the horse is not going forwards and is lacking energy and holding back. He should be made to answer the leg aids promptly and wake up.

Canter broken This is intended to mean that the correct three beats of the canter is not true but it can also mean a horse cantering 'croup high'. These horses are not going forwards properly or have learned to evade collection by putting their hindquarters up instead of lowering them thus interfering with the purity of the gait.

Croup high See 'canter broken'. Horses that have learned to evade their riders in this way are tiresome as they stiffen their back, and will resist any leg aids that are given to make them go forwards.

NOVICE STANDARD TEST

No   **Horse**   **Rider**

Test	Marks Max	Judge's Marks	Observations
1 A Enter at working trot X Halt. Salute. Proceed at working trot	10	2 5	Fairly straight in entry. Resisted to halt. $\frac{1}{4}$'s swing.
2 C Track left E Circle left 15 m diameter A Working trot	10	6	Active trot but lacking bend.
3 F to M Working trot. Give and re-take the reins M Working trot	10	5	Lost rhythm and resistance in re-take.
4 C Working canter left A Circle left 20 m diameter M Working trot	10	7	
5 C. Halt. Immobility 4 seconds Proceed in medium walk	10	4	Abrupt halt. Not square and resistance.
6 H–B Change rein at free walk on a long rein B Medium walk	10	7	
7 F Working trot E Circle right 15 m diameter	10	6	Lacking impulsion.
8 H Working canter C Circle right 20 m diameter	10	7	
9 F Working trot K–H Give and re-take the reins	10	5	Loss of balance and rhythm.
10 MXK Change the rein in working trot showing a few lengthened strides A Turn down centre G Halt. Salute, Leave the arena in free walk at A	10	6	Quite good lengthened strides but some resistance in transition at K. Fairly straight till halt then quarters slightly to left.
11 General impression, obedience and calmness	10	5	Try to improve submission to the aids especially in transitions.
12 Paces and impulsion	10	6	Better engagement of the hindquarters would keep the balance and enable the horse to hold his rhythm.
13 Position and seat of rider and correct application of the aids	10	6	Sympathetically ridden. In places better preparation would have improved the movement.
Total	130	77	

Total of column 2
Faults to be deducted

Judge's signature *Janet Smith*

An example of a dressage score sheet. The judge's writer has to write in longhand and keep up with the test – hence you may encounter some rather unusual abbreviations!

Scale of marks

10 Excellent		Approx time 4½ mins
9 Very good		
8 Good		Errors over the course are penalised:
7 Fairly good		
6 Satisfactory		
5 Sufficient		First error 2 points
4 Insufficient		Second error 4 points
3 Fairly bad		Third error 8 points
2 Bad		Fourth error Elimination
1 Very bad		
0 Not performed		N.b. Penalties are accumulative

Cutting corners Mainly novice riders allow their horses to do this, which means that they do not ride into the corners properly, thus wasting a good deal of space. In so doing they are not in a position to begin movements properly. It is a slovenly way to ride and denotes an unknowledgeable or lazy rider!

Falling in Another rider failing I am afraid, as it means that when the horse is travelling round the school his rider is allowing him to lean over like a motorbike! Instead of staying on the track or describing proper curves, he takes the weight on his inside shoulder and hindquarter, thus making him unbalanced.

Falling out This fault occurs mainly on circles or turns, when instead of following the line accurately, the horse sways outwards, taking the weight onto his outside shoulder. The outside aids of his rider are not sufficiently effective.

Four time This wording is probably quite clear in context as it has to do with the canter gait being the wrong sequence. Usually the cause is lack of impulsion which allows the horse to stay close to the ground instead of showing a moment of suspension.

Hollow outline This relates to the shape made by the horse when he is asked to come on the aids but evades by putting his head and sometimes his croup high thus making his back look as though it has sunk. A good outline is one which is rounded with the horse going forwards, accepting the combined use of leg and hand without resistance.

Insufficient angle This remark would normally be associated with the angle of the shoulder-in which should be about 30° from the line upon which the horse is travelling, i.e. the side of the school or the centre line. Other remarks regarding difficulties in shoulder-in may be made, such as 'losing angle' when it is gradually reducing, or 'varying angle' when it is changing from 30° to less than that or even to more.

Insufficient bend Some riders do not seem to be aware of the degree of bend required in various movements. For example, the degree needed for a ten-metre circle must necessarily be greater than that for a 20-metre circle. Also, the amount of bend for a half pass will vary according to the degree of angle. Another point is that a bend should be a true curve from one end of the horse to the other. A bend in the neck only is often mistaken for a bend in the horse but this is false and will be marked down. A true bend is when the horse, responding correctly to the aids, curves himself uniformly round his rider's inside leg.

Insufficient engagement The horse's hindquarters have not been brought under his body putting him in a position of being able to be balanced, collected and impulsive.

Irregular This word crops up rather often, unfortunately, as it affects the marks seriously. Instead of the horse making deliberate, consistent steps in a well-maintained rhythm, there is variation either for a few steps at a time or for a prolonged period. There may be a number of causes, including a fault in the horse's speed, balance or acceptance of the aids. Whatever the reason, make sure that any irregular steps are eradicated.

Lacking activity Activity relates to the bending of the joints of the hind legs which should come well under the horse.

Lacking freedom This does not mean that the rider should in any way release the rein contact although it may be that the contact is too firm and thus restrictive to the horse's gaits or outline. A lightening of the contact may be needed in order to allow the horse to round himself, take a bigger and more ground-covering stride. This lightening can only occur as a result of correct balance, suppleness and obedience to the aids. To allow freedom does not mean that the horse can do as he likes, but merely gives the opportunity for the gaits to be unconstrained.

Lacking height The use of this term is made during the passage to indicate that the lift is not sufficient. More engagement and impulsion are needed, combined with collection and submission.

Lacking impulsion Riders often misunderstand impulsion and sometimes think that they merely have to speed up to achieve it whereas true impulsion is energy created by engaging the hindquarters through acceptance of the hand and leg which then takes the horse forwards with rhythmic, springing steps.

Late behind This remark refers to the flying changes and means that instead of the horse bringing his hind leg forwards at the same moment as his foreleg during the change it comes through later. This is often caused by lack of engagement and impulsion but also from lack of collection and a proper moment of suspension during which the change should occur.

Neck too short This comment evolved because some riders mistakenly try to collect their horse by too much use of the hand causing the neck to raise and draw back, often resulting in overbending and restriction.

Not enough difference In a test where there is a variety within the gaits (working, medium and/or extended) it is important to show clear differences between one and the other, not only because it is correct training but also to leave no doubt in the judge's mind as to what is supposed to be happening.

Not going forwards This sounds as though the horse should go faster but in fact it means that the horse should be more active and impulsive and covering more ground on a bigger, more springing stride.

Not in diagonals This remark might be used during a piaffe, where the horse, having lost his impulsion and attention to the aids tries to shuffle with his feet into a four-time beat instead of marking time with one pair of diagonal legs and then the other as for trot.

On the forehand There are many riders who still allow their horses to take their weight on their forehand, which inhibits freedom of the shoulders and restricts the gait. It is not easy to learn to engage the hindquarters but it is the only way to improve balance and reduce the ugly labouring of a horse on his forehand who will never be a pleasant ride or able to progress beyond a very limited point.

Pivoted This word might be used during a pirouette to indicate that instead of the gait remaining correct, the sequence has been lost as the horse swivels on one or both hind feet. The word 'stuck' is sometimes used meaning the same thing. This will happen if the horse stops going forwards.

Quarters in   This simply means that the horse is evading being straight or being correctly bent by curving his hindquarters round the rider's inside leg so that the hind feet do not follow the forefeet. It is most likely to occur during transitions and on the long side of the school. Horses will tend to put their quarters in on one rein more than the other due to unequal suppleness. Shoulder-in position is the proper way to correct the problem.

Resisting   This remark occurs frequently in tests and applies to any horse who is disobedient to the aids or shows objection in any way. If a horse is taken by surprise, caught off balance or upset, he will show some resistance.

Running   Describes the scrabbling action resulting from hurrying the stride and allowing the weight to be on the forehand. It happens during the lengthening of the trot, when the rider is endeavouring to show a difference but has allowed the horse to become unbalanced and out of rhythm.

Tilting head (tipping head)   The horse will angle his head on his neck instead of carrying it straight thus enabling him to avoid equal pressure of the bit and consequently the aids. Tilting the head is a wonderful way for the horse to get out of bending properly and often happens as the work becomes harder and more is required of him. To deal with the problem, the rider should check the correct effect of his aids.

Tongue out   This occurs at all levels but perhaps more frequently in the higher tests. It is basically an evasion to the aids, but in all probability incorrectly fitted bits (especially the double bridle bits) may have triggered off the problem. If the tongue is not in the mouth, the bit or bits cannot be brought to bear. Any evasion of them will lose marks in a test.

Turn on the centre   When a pirouette is incorrectly executed, the hind feet describing a tiny half circle or circle, with the forefeet describing a larger one, sometimes the horse will swing his hindquarters out which is described as a turn on the centre. He should be made more attentive to the aids but in particular to the outside leg.

Uneven   Sometimes this comment has to be used to describe steps which do not match each other for a brief moment. The cause may be the ground or a slight loss of balance but it is not considered to be as sinister as the following word.

Unlevel   This is generally a polite way of saying that the horse looks unsound! On rare occasions a horse is quite obviously lame and has to be asked to leave the arena, but on others he just does not look quite right. It may be for a few strides or it may be so slight that it is merely a suspicion. At any rate anything that looks suspect may be regarded as unlevel. If you get this comment do check it out as it will lose you many marks and could be causing the horse damage.

Wide behind   This can happen in halt, rein back or any lengthening or extension in trot. The cause is generally due to incorrect engagement of the hindquarters, possibly due to rigidity in the horse's back or mouth. Not only is it unattractive but also is a deviation from the purity of the gait when the hind feet should follow the track of the forefeet. It is a clever resistance by the horse as the rider is often unaware of its existence. Loss of balance or leaning on the hand can bring this about.

28
RULES AND REGULATIONS

It would be impossible to mention all the rules in this text but here are some general guidelines to follow which I hope will be helpful.

First of all, it is important to present yourself correctly for the specific test you wish to ride, so from your National Rules find out exactly what dress is required (see also page 134). It may be a rule that a hat must be worn even when riding in so be sure of this point.

The horse must wear the correct bridle, for the test. Only certain bits are allowed (see Figure 70). Saddles are to suit the rider. Sometimes saddle cloths are allowed. Boots or bandages, martingales, side or running reins and blinkers are not permitted in tests in any case but also the warming up may have to be done in the permitted saddlery only. Lungeing may be done in a cavesson with one or two reins and side reins. Fines or elimination can result from breaches of the permitted tack.

Points to Note

- Horses must only be entered for classes for which they are eligible. Height certificates may be required for ponies if they wish to compete in classes requiring them to be 14.2hh and under.
- Riders and horses/ponies have to be registered with their National Association and fees paid up to date.
- No stimulants or sedatives may be given to horse or rider and tests may be made to check on this fact.
- When at the show do not enter the arena before the signal to start. When the signal has gone, you have 60 seconds to enter the arena.
- You may or may not be allowed a 'commander' to read out the test, so check this.
- If you take the wrong direction a signal will be made by the judge at which point you should go to him/her to be told from where to carry on. Marks will be deducted.
- Taking the wrong direction four times means elimination.
- A movement begins when the rider's body is next to a marker.
- During the salute riders must take the reins in one hand. If a whip is carried, it should be held in the rein hand.
- Riders must leave the arena at A after finishing a test.
- Leaving the arena during a test constitutes elimination if the arena board is 23 cm (9 in) high or more, otherwise if the horse leaves the arena, no marks will be given for that movement.

- Riders should not dismount for any reason during a test. In the case of a fall, they may remount and continue but the movement will be penalised.
- Any horse refusing to go forwards for a period of 20 seconds during a test will be eliminated.
- Grinding the teeth and tail swishing are signs of nervousness or resistance and will be penalised.
- The use of the voice is not permitted during a test.
- The judge will use a marking sheet for putting down the marks and remarks.

The competitors will be given their mark sheets at the end of the competition.

Anyone trying to aid a rider by voice or signs from outside the arena would be considered to be giving outside assistance and would cause the rider to be eliminated.

KEEP UP TO DATE WITH RULES

There are specific rules sometimes for a particular competition but keep up to date with all rules and rule changes so that you are not caught out.

Nothing is more heartbreaking than to have prepared for and travelled miles to a show only to be eliminated for something which could have been avoided.

29

FINAL ANALYSIS

Throughout this book, emphasis has been upon what the rider wants from the horse and how to obtain it. In this concluding chapter I should like to draw attention to the other half of the equation, namely the horse, and to give some consideration to his desires or needs.

Looking After Your Horse

In as much as we care and look after our horse, it is human nature to expect him to do what we want for a short period each day. It is this co-operation that is worth thinking about for a moment and deciding whether we as riders are worthy of the horse's willingness to oblige us. Do we do our best to make work pleasurable for him? Do we make proper allowances for misunderstandings, for physical disadvantages, for youth, for old age, for lack of fitness, for stiffness, lameness, for the ground we ride on, for nervousness and anxiety? Do we deal with temper tantrums in the right way and can we be patient with the illogical idiosyncrasies which crop up with some horses? Do we make ourselves clear? Are we consistent? Do we follow a system or are we haphazard and frequently changing our ideas?

I believe that we are all guilty of having, at some time in our riding career, misused the trust we wish the horse to have in us. We have let him down, probably from ignorance or thoughtlessness. Riding can certainly be an art but even those who merely want to enjoy themselves have a responsibility to the horse they profess to worship. How often do we abuse our horses for the sake of competition? Some riders, hopefully in the minority, will do anything to win a prize and sometimes the horse suffers torture in their endeavour to achieve their aim. Riders expect the horse to respond to their will whether they are ready or not and this clearly is not right. Much mental preparation is necessary on the part of the rider, in-depth study of the subject, a plan of action followed by patient, systematic application. Common sense plays a big part in the scheme but horse-sense and logical preparation is better.

Competition is very demanding for horse and rider, and unfortunately, the dedicated competitor has to learn to compromise sometimes the feel he would like for the accuracy demanded by the test.

Some riders will dislike this compromise and almost be unable to bring themselves to accept less than the feel they know they can obtain in training. A dressage test, however, is there to be ridden as laid down and although all competition riders hope that their feel for

29 A top dressage horse and rider – Margitt Otto-Crepin on Corlandus

what is right may actually come off in the test, they know that if it is mislaid they must grin and bear it and do the best they can. If the training has been classical, this situation should arise less often as the horse will be ready for what he has to do. If there is a flaw in the training, tension enters the picture as the rider battles to cover mistakes and faults. This is when untidy or rough aids can spoil the performance, and the horse, struggling himself, has to cope with his own problems as well as those of his rider. The whole object of dressage as an art is lost. A rider who starts with a lovely horse and then, by tactless or uninformed training, destroys it, should be very ashamed.

Those riders who have horses with good conformation and gaits are half way there but those with lesser animals may do well if they do not expect the impossible and will train with patience. It is no good expecting more of your horse than he is physically capable of giving. He will do his best, but if he has a conformation defect, do not expect that even good training will necessarily counteract the difficulty.

A horse has an astounding memory and if properly taught he will never forget. (A good 'schoolmaster' can go through a test sometimes in spite of his rider!) It is imperative to use this attribute and thoroughly confirm by systematic work what you want the horse to remember. He will learn by repetition and reward. This does not mean boring him by doing the same thing for hours. It means repeating an exercise until there is some improvement, however small, and then praising him with a pat on the neck. Rest periods are essential in training sessions, not only for physical reasons but also from the point of view of giving the brain an opportunity to absorb the work.

When things go wrong, go back to the beginning and start again. When they go right, give much praise. Through sympathy and companionship attain your goal and at the end your horse will be as proud and happy as you are with the result **(29)**.

APPENDIXES: SAMPLE TESTS

TEST AT NOVICE LEVEL

The following pages are a guide and some of the movements used in tests at the different levels of training and the requirements and points upon which judges will be directing their attention.

Example of a test at Novice level and requirements

	Entry in working trot	Straightness on centre line
	Halt – Salute – Proceed in working trot	Smoothness of transitions. Immobility in halt
C	Track right	Correct bend
FD	Half circle right 10 m diameter returning to the track balance at M	Correct bend rhythm and Accuracy of half-circle. Quality of trot, i.e. activity and impression, regularity and outline
C	Serpentine three loops each loop to touch the side of the arena	As above
F	Working centre left	Smoothness of transition
B	Circle left 20 m	Accuracy. Quality of centre, i.e. correct canter sequence of steps. Balance, bend, rhythm impression and outline
M	Working trot	Transition – smooth and free from resistance
C	Medium walk	Transition as above
HXF	Change rein at free walk on long rein	Smooth swing and taking up of rein. Good stretching downwards of head and neck. Hindfeet overtracking imprint of forefeet

F	Medium walk	Acceptance of aids from free walk. Activity of walk and outline
A	Working trot	Smooth transition
K	Working canter	As above
E	Circle right 20 m diameter	Quality of canter. Bend, rhythm, balance and outline
H	Working trot	The transition
MXK	Change rein and show a few lengthened strides	Straightness. Quality of lengthening. Transition to and from lengthening
A	Turn down centre line	Bend on the turn. Straightness. The transition into halt. Immobility
G	Halt. Salute	

TEST AT ELEMENTARY LEVEL

Example of an Elementary standard test

A	Enter at working trot	Straightness
X	Halt – Salute	Transition. Immobility
C	Track right	Bend
MXK	Change rein at medium trot	Amount of difference. Quality of steps
A	Down centre line	Bend and balance on turn
Between D&K	Circle left 10 m diameter	Suppleness. Rhythm and regularity. Outline
Between X&G	Circle right 10 m diameter	As above and equality of circles to each other
C	Track right	
B	Halt. Immobility 4 seconds Proceed at working trot	Transition. Immobility
A	Medium walk	Quality of steps. Regularity
KXM	Change rein at medium walk	
C	Working centre left (directly from walk)	Transition
E	Circle left 15 m diameter	Suppleness. Outline. Balance. Rhythm
FMC	Medium canter	Difference shown in Transitions
C	Working canter	
K	Half circle left 10 m diameter	Bend. Balance. Ease of movement
H	Working trot	Quality
C	Working canter right	Transition

B	Circle right 15 m diameter	Suppleness. Outline. Balance. Rhythm
KHC	Medium canter	Difference shown
C	Working canter	Transition
F	Half circle right 10 m diameter returning to the track at B	Bend. Balance. Ease of movement
M	Working trot	Transition
HXF	Change rein in medium trot	Difference shown. Balance. Transitions
A	Down centre line	
G	Halt. Salute	Straightness. Transitions. Immobility

TEST AT MEDIUM LEVEL

Example of a Medium standard test

A	Enter at collected canter	Straightness
X	Halt. Immobility. Salute. Proceed at collected trot	Transitions. Immobility Collection
C	Track. Track left	Quality of turn
HXF	Change rein medium trot	Difference between collection and medium regularity
F	Collected trot	Transitions
H	Half pirouette right. Proceed at collected trot	Balance. Bend. Size of pirouette. Activity
EK	Shoulder-in left	Suppleness. Angle
A	Circle left 7 m diameter	Suppleness. Size of circle
FB	Travers	Suppleness. Angle. Correctness of movement. Regularity
BMHE	Collected trot	Collection
K	Half pirouette left	Balance. Bend. Size. Activity
EH	Shoulder-in right	Suppleness. Angle
C	Circle right 7 m diameter	Suppleness. Size of circle
HB	Travers	Suppleness. Angle. Regularity of steps
A	Halt. Rein back 4 steps	Outline. Quantity of steps. Correct number of steps. Straightness
	Proceed in collected canter right	Transition
KEH	Medium canter	Difference between medium and collection. Transition
HCM	Collected canter	

MX	Half pass right	Suppleness
X	Collected walk to D	Collection. Activity
D	Collected canter left	Directness of transition
A	Track left	
FX	Half pass left	Suppleness. Quality of canter
X	Continue down centre line	Straightness
C	Turn left	
HEK	Medium canter	Difference between medium and collection
K	Collected canter	Transition
A	Medium walk	Activity and regularity
FXH	Change rein extended walk	Quality of extension
H	Collected walk	Collection
C	Collected canter	Directness of transition
MBA	Collected canter	Collection and straightness
AEH	Extended canter	Quality of extension
H	Collected canter	Transitions
C	Collected trot	Transitions
MXK	Extended trot	Balance and quality of extension
K	Collected trot	Transitions
A	Turn down centre	Balance and suppleness of turn
X	Halt. Immobility. Salute	Straightness. Transitions. Immobility

MOVEMENTS AT HIGHER LEVELS

Other movements

Advanced Medium	Changes in the air. Counter canter (greater difficulty)
Lower Advanced Tests	Half pirouettes in canter. Counter change of hand in trot and canter. Tempi-changes to three time
Advanced tests and FEI	Full canter-pirouettes. Zig-Zags in trot and canter. Rein back see-saw. Tempi-changes to one time. Piaffe. Passage.

As the severity of tests increase, judges are primarily concerned with a specific movement being performed. However, throughout the whole process assessment of basic requirements will also be made and, of course, without the quality of these, all movements are likely to be adversely affected. In all tests the judge will be taking the exit from the arena at A into account and will also be marking the gaits (paces), the impulsion, the submission and the riders at the end of each test.

The special qualities looked for regarding the gaits are correctness of the sequence of steps, regularity, rhythm, balance, freedom and willingness to go forward.

The impulsion section is the energy, activity, elasticity of steps, suppleness and engagement of the hind-quarters.

Submission means the willingness with which the horse co-operates to the aids, his confidence, calmness and lightness of the forehand and ease of performing movements in harmony with his rider.

The rider is marked on his position and ability to maintain it whether he gives the aids effectively, but unobtrusively and whether he can control the horse to such a degree that he can show all movements clearly and can ride an accurate test.

TEST AT FIFTH LEVEL (USA)

Example of test at fifth level, USA

A	Enter collected canter		M	Turn right
X	Halt, salute, proceed collected trot		Between G and H	Half pirouette right
C	Track left		Between G and M	Half pirouette left
HK	Medium trot		G	Collected canter right
K	Collected trot		H	Turn right
FX	Half pass left		MF	Medium canter
X	Votte left 6 m		F	Collected canter
XG	Shoulder-in left		KX	Half pass right
C	Track left		X	Flying change of lead
E	Turn left		XH	Half pass left
X	Halt. Rein back 5 steps. Proceed in collected trot		H	Flying change of lead
B	Turn right		HMX	Collected canter
KX	Half pass right		Between M and X	Half pirouette right
X	Volte right 6 m		M	Flying change
XG	Shoulder-in right		MHX	Collected canter
C	Track right		Between H and X	Half pirouette left
MXK	Change rein extended trot		H	Flying change
K	Collected trot		MXK	5 flying changes of lead every fourth stride
A	Medium walk			
FXH	Extended walk			
H	Collected walk			

FXK	5 flying changes of lead every third stride	K	Collected canter and flying change
MXK	Change rein in extended canter	A	Down centre line
		G	Halt. Salute

TEST AT INTERNATIONAL LEVEL FOR PONIES

A	Enter in collected canter
X	Halt. Salute. Proceed in collected trot
C	Track to the left
SK	Medium trot
K	Collected trot
FB	Shoulder-in
BX	Half circle left 10 m
XE	Half circle right 10 m
EH	Shoulder-in
HCBF	Collected trot
F	Half circle right 10 m
DR	Half pass right
C.	Halt. Rein back 5 steps. Proceed in collected trot
RCEK	Collected trot
K	Half circle left 10 m
DS	Half pass left
MXK	Change rein in extended trot
K	Collected trot
A	Medium walk
FXH	Change rein in extended walk
H	Collected walk
C	Proceed in collected canter right
MF	Medium canter
F	Collected canter
A	On centre line
X	Simple change of leg
C	Track right
CR	Counter canter
RV	Change rein without change of leg
A	Simple change of leg
PV	Half-circle in counter canter
K	Collected walk
P	Half pirouette to the left
V	Half pirouette to the right
A	Proceed in collected canter
FM	Medium canter
M	Collected canter
HXF	Change rein in extended canter
F	Collected canter
A	On centre line
X	Halt. Salute

FURTHER READING

The following are just a few of the many books that the dressage student may find of use and interest.

Early masters

XENOPHON, *The Art of Horsemanship*, Ed. Morris H. Morgan, J.A. Allen

Dressage

CROSSLEY, A., *Dressage, The Seat, Aids and Exercises*, Pelham Books, 1988 (UK), Viking Penguin (US)
LOCH, S., *Dressage, The Art of Classical Riding*, The Sportsman's Press, 1990 (UK), Trafalgar Square Publishing (US)
LORISTON-CLARKE, J., *Complete Guide to Dressage*, S. Paul, 1990 (UK), Running Press (US)
MARSHALL, L., *Questions of Dressage*, J.A. Allen, 1989
PODHAJSKY, A., *Complete Training of Horse and Rider*, Pelham, 1991 (UK), Doubleday (US)

Dressage Competition

BURTON, J., *How To Ride A Winning Dressage Test*, Houghton Mifflin, 1985 (US)
GAHWYLER, M., *The Competitive Edge*, Half-Halt Press, 1990 (US)
MARSHALL, L., *Dressage Terms*, J.A. Allen, 1980

Dressage to music

CAMPBELL, M., *Dancing With Your Horse*, Half-Halt Press, 1989 (US)
MACDONALD, J., *Riding to Music*, J.A. Allen, 1987

Young riders

HENRIQUES, P., *Dressage for the Young Rider*, Threshold Books, 1990 (UK), Half-Halt Press (US)

Videos

Understanding Dressage – featuring David Hunt
Dr Reiner Klimke Training Series
The Art of Riding Series
Centred Riding Parts I & II

Feeding and Fitness

HODGES, J., & Pilliner, S., *The Equine Athlete, How to Develop Your Horse's Athletic Potential*, Blackwell Scientific, 1992 (UK), Trafalgar Square Publishing (US)
LAUNDERS, E. & LUCAS, D., *Feeding Facts,* Horse and Rider (UK)
PILLINER, S., *Getting Horses Fit*, Blackwell Scientific, 1987 (UK), Sheridan (US)
TUKE, D., *Getting Your Horse Fit*, J.A. Allen, 1977
WAGONER, D., ed., *Feeding To Win II*, Equine Research, 1992 (US)

Lungeing and longreining

INDERWICK, S., *Lungeing The Horse and Rider*, David & Charles, 1977, (UK), Trafalgar Square Publishing (US)

KARL, P., *Long Reining*, A & C Black, 1992, (UK), Trafalgar Square Publishing (US)

STANIER, S., *The Art of Lungeing*, J.A. Allen, 1976

STANIER, S., *The Art of Longreining*, J.A. Allen, 1986

Rider's approach/attitude

SAVOIE, J., *That Winning Feeling!*, J.A. Allen, 1992, (UK), Trafalgar Square Publishing, (US)

SWIFT, S., *Centred Riding*, Kingswood, 1985, (UK), Trafalgar Square Publishing (US)

WANLESS, M., *Ride With Your Mind*, Methuen, 1987/US title: *The Natural Rider*, Trafalgar Square Publishing

WANLESS, M., *Ride With Your Mind Masterclass*, Methuen, 1991, (UK), Trafalgar Square Publishing, (US)

Addresses

UK

The Dressage Group
The British Horse Society
British Equestrian Centre
Kenilworth
Warwickshire
CV8 2LR

USA

American Horse Shows Association
220 East 42nd Street
New York NY 10017

United States Dressage Federation
P.O. Box 80668
Lincoln, NE 68501–0668

INDEX